# CALL
## OF THE
## CHAIR

Leading the Board
of the Christ-centered Ministry

David L. McKenna

# DEDICATION

Dedicated

to

Board Chairs

with Whom I Served

**********

Hugh White

Glenn White

Paul Walls

Forest Bush

Ira Gallaway

Maxie Dunnam

# TABLE OF CONTENTS

## Part III – Artistry of the Chair

# FOREWORD

This book fills a long-standing need.

The board's approach to selecting its chair speaks volumes about the importance the board places on this key position. Moreover, the quality of the chair selection process may well determine the effectiveness of the board.

Whatever the process, without the call of God upon the board chair, we cannot expect the board chair to give the task the highest priority of time, energy, and resources.

Is the board chair *just another* board position—an equal among equals? Hardly!

The board chair must be *first* among equals. Why? As David McKenna says, "Underlying the professional qualifications for the board chair are three sensitive areas of board leadership that depend directly on personal character: Integrity, trust, and humility."

- The board chair must be first among equals in *integrity*. While every board member must possess high moral and ethical standards, the character of the board chair is the most visible. The ministry's top leader is the public face of the organization, but the chair is the face of the board.

- The board chair must be first among equals in *trust*. The board chair must also have the gift of diplomacy. Yet, more important than diplomacy is the gift of building relationships based on trust—relationships with the ministry's top leader, the entire board, the standing committees, the task forces, and each individual member.

- The board chair must be first among equals in *humility*. The title of board chair has a lofty sound, yet the title comes with no inherent authority or power. It is only the board itself which authorizes the chair to speak or act on its behalf.

The board chair may be the holder of a lofty title, wielder of a ready gavel, collaborator with the CEO, announcer of good and bad news, voice of the board, or the power behind the scene. No matter how the board chair is described, it is the key position of the board.

Thank you, David, for writing a book that will serve Christ-centered ministries and their boards for many years to come!

Dan Busby
President
ECFA

# PART I

---

## AUTHORITY
## OF THE CHAIR

# FIRST AMONG EQUALS

Do you remember the fable of the blind men describing an elephant by their touch? According to their reports, an elephant is an ivory tusk, a spiny tail, a floppy ear, a leathery trunk, or a massive foot. They needed sight to see the whole animal.

The chair of the board is subject to the same piecemeal descriptions. Depending on the place where the role is touched, the board chair may be the holder of a lofty title, wielder of a ready gavel, collaborator with the chief executive, announcer of good and bad news, signer of contracts, voice of the board, or power behind the scene.

Like the blind men's touch, each of these descriptions may be partially true, but none is complete in itself. A full picture of the role of the board chair is needed, especially for Christ-centered institutions where wholeness includes the spiritual dimension in any job description.

## A Personal Perspective

Experience qualifies me to look at the role of the chair of the Christ-centered organization from a perspective in which the parts become the whole. Thirty-three consecutive years as president of Spring Arbor College (now University), Seattle Pacific College (now University), and Asbury Theological Seminary, serving under three different boards of trustees, and working in close relationship with their respective chairs are the credentials I bring to write on the subject. Later on, I served as chair of the board for Spring Arbor University and as founding chair for the new Bakke Graduate University. Quite naturally, then, I was called to consult with the boards of such institutions as Wheaton College, Seattle University, Messiah College, and Asbury University. Add the years as a board member for civic organizations, such as United Way of the Bluegrass; educational associations, such as the National Association of Independent Colleges and Universities; national associations, such as the National Association of Evangelicals; and international organizations, such as the World Methodist Council.

With eyes wide open, I have witnessed the role of board chair from every angle. Let my career in Christian higher education serve as an example:

- As a student in a Christian college, I was awed by the chair of the board as a symbol of authority;

- as a faculty member at the same college, the chair was a man of mystery functioning behind closed doors;

- as president of the same institution, I realized that my survival depended upon a relationship of mutual trust with the chair;

- as chair of the same board, I learned the leverage as well as the limits of the role; and finally,

- as a consultant to the same board, I learned how much a growing board depends upon a chair who is called to the position, elected according to established criteria, and held accountable for performance in the role.

None of these parts is adequate to describe the full role of the chair of the board, but put together, they set the stage for seeing a portrait of the whole as well as snapshots of the parts.

## A Professional Perspective

Bylaws and board manuals spell out the authority and responsibility of the board chair as the voluntary leader of the governing board. These descriptions vary from a simple statement of title and task to a complex set of expectations and relationships. To show this progression from the simple to the complex, imagine the role of the chair rising through these levels of responsibility, compiled from professional resources and applied to Christ-centered ministries. *Note:* The following descriptions of the role of the board chair are compiled from a variety of institutional and professions sources and composed according to my experience and understanding of the position from the standpoint of the Christ-centered ministry.

**I. Legal Authority.** Bylaws of for-profit and nonprofit corporations mandate the board to elect a chair, vice chair, secretary, and treasurer as corporate officers. The chair's authority is also spelled out in leadership of the board structure:

The chair is the senior volunteer leader of the organization elected by the Board of Trustees who presides at all meetings of the Board, the Executive Committee and other meetings as required. The Chair is an ex officio member of all committees of the organization. The Board Chair oversees implementation of board and organizational policies and ensures that appropriate administrative practices are established and maintained.

The length of the chair's term of office is a variable that ranges from one year to a lifetime. With a view toward balancing limited tenure with leadership continuity, the current movement is toward term limits ranging from three to six years.

**II. Primary Functions.** A listing of leadership functions for the board chair is not common in the bylaws of corporations. The list is often reserved for an operating manual or inferred from a statement of basic functions for the full board according to the standards of good practice in board governance. When viewing these primary functions, it is most important to see the connection between the leadership responsibility of the chair and the primary functions of the board itself. The chair has no functions that are not conferred by the board and supportive of board responsibilities. With this caveat in mind, we understand that the role of the chair is to lead the board in the achievement of these outcomes:

- Determining mission and purpose

- Selecting the chief executive

- Supporting and evaluating the chief executive

- Ensuring effective planning

- Monitoring and strengthening programs and services

- Ensuring adequate financial resources

- Protecting assets and assuring proper financial oversight

- Building a competent board

- Ensuring legal and ethical integrity

- Enhancing public standing of the organization

**III. Leadership Qualifications.** To perform the functions required of the board chair, a candidate must bring both character and competency to the role. As the principles of leadership development are applied to all levels of management in our organizations, the qualifications for the board chair need to be specifically outlined in official documents. Following is a list of competencies expected for a board chair:

1. Personal integrity and public credibility;

2. Passionate commitment and understanding of the organizational mission;

3. Executive leadership accomplishments in business, government, religion, philanthropy, or the nonprofit sector;

4. Service in a leadership position of the board (e.g., committee chair or executive committee member);

5. Earned respect of board members, chief executive, and key stakeholders;

6. Diplomatic skills in building relationships, handling conflict, and building consensus;

7. Communication skills, oral and written, with an ability to listen, elicit diverse responses, reconcile differences, and

8. Willingness and ability to commit time to leadership of the organization.

**IV. Operational Duties.** When the basic functions of board leadership come together with the qualifications for the board chair, a specific set of operational expectations follow. The board chair is expected to:

1. Guide and direct the governance process, centering the work of the board on the organization's mission, vision, and strategic direction;

2. Establish agendas for board and executive committee meetings in collaboration with the president or executive director;

3. Preside over board and executive committee meetings in a manner that encourages participation and information sharing while moving the board toward timely closure and prudent decision-making;

4. Appoint committee chairs and members, subject to board approval;

5. Work with committee chairpersons to align the work of committees with the vision and goals of the ministry;

6. Serve as the board's central point of official communication with the chief executive;

7. Develop a positive, collaborative relationship with the chief executive, including acting as a sounding board for the chief executive on emerging issues and alternative courses of action;

8. Stay up-to-date about the organization and determine when an issue needs to be brought to the attention of the full board or a committee;

9. Lead the processes of goal-setting, performance evaluation, and compensation review for the chief executive consistent with board policy;

10. Serve as an ex officio member of all committees;

11. Set a high standard for board conduct by modeling, articulating, and upholding rules of conduct set out in board bylaws and policies. Intervene when necessary in instances involving conflict of interest, confidentiality, and other board policies;

12. Participate in the recruitment of new board members;

13. Play a central role in orientation of new board members, mentoring a chair-elect, and providing continuing education for the entire board;

14. Provide for an effective, objective board self-evaluation process and support implementation of recommendations for improvement. Seek feedback on his or her performance as chairperson.

**V. Leadership Assessment.** Few boards require assessment of the performance of their chair according to the expectations of the task description. More often, board members breathe a sigh of relief and wipe their brows because someone is willing to serve as chair. As leadership development becomes an expectation at every level of the organization, however, the board chair needs to be included in some kind of formal assessment. The time is now.

Board chairs should be assessed on a schedule coordinated with their election or term of office, according to the general and specific functions outlined for their position. Outside consultation may or may not be included. Review of the performance of the board chair begins with a self-assessment that is combined with a review by a governance committee and presented to the full board as the basis for reelection or recognition upon retirement. Assessment need not be elaborate or laborious. To start, ask how effective the board chair is in:

- Understanding and articulating the chartered mission and strategic vision of the ministry.

- Partnering with the chief executive in a climate of mutual trust in order to lead in developing and enacting policies consistent with the goals of the organization.

- Building a board known for its professional culture, relational climate, representative diversity, developmental initiative, honest assessment, and consensus action.

- Assuring the good will of stakeholders—constituency groups, donors, friends, and the general public—who support the mission of the ministry.

# First among Equals

Our review of the authority, functions, qualifications, and assessment for the board chair leads us to stop and reflect on the meaning of this section's title, "First among Equals." Underlying the professional qualifications for the board chair are three sensitive areas of board leadership that depend directly on personal character. Succinctly stated, it is expected that the board chair of an organization—whether secular or religious—is a person of integrity, trust, and humility. I have named these expectations "bridge qualities" because they reach out from the standards of good practice in a secular organization to the virtues of spiritual maturity in the Christ-centered ministry. Starting on the secular side of the bridge, we see these qualities undergirding the standards of good practice.

## First among Equals in Integrity

The board chair must be first among equals in integrity. Although every trustee or director has to qualify on moral and ethical standards, it is the chair whose character is most visible and accountable. As the president or executive director is the public face of the organization, the chair is the public face of the board. When he or she speaks or acts with the conferred power of the board, the credibility of the organization is on the line. Behind the public face must stand the demonstrated evidence of personal integrity. Whether the organization is religious or secular, profit or nonprofit—there can be no compromise. Personal integrity and public credibility are the indispensable qualities of character that determine whether or not the board chair can develop the internal and external relationships required of the role.

# First among Equals in Trust

In close companionship with integrity, the chair is first among equals in trust. Diplomacy is the skill required of the chair to invite dialogue, handle conflict, and arrive at consensus. But deeper than diplomacy is the gift of building relationships based on trust, with none more demanding than the chair–chief executive relationship. The Board Policy Manual of Asbury Theological Seminary leaves no doubt about its importance:

> The board chair manages the board while the president manages the Seminary. The relationship between board chair and Seminary president, however, is symbiotic and mutually supportive. The chair seeks input from the president on managing the board, while the president seeks input from the chair on managing the Seminary. The importance of the relationship between the board chair and the Seminary president cannot be underestimated.

The same level of trust determines the quality of the chair's relationships with the whole board, its working committees, and each individual member. The trust that underlies these relationships must be earned, not just through diplomatic skills, but in company with the virtues of personal integrity and public credibility.

## First among Equals in Humility

The chair is first among equals in humility for the authority conferred by his or her peers on the board. From reading the leadership functions of the chair, we might conclude that the position is high-powered and self-contained. Nothing could be farther from the truth. The title of chair comes with no inherent authority or power. Only as the board itself authorizes the chair to speak or act on its behalf is he or she different from any other member. Even the legal authority to sign contacts, notes, bonds, certificates, and other papers is annually conferred to the chair by the board. With humility, the chair accepts the limits of the role and avoids the arrogance of corrupting power. A chair who goes beyond the specific authorization of the board is abusing the position and its limited power.

The role of the board chair that we have described generally applies to the position in any organization—for-profit, nonprofit, or Christ-centered. The difference is not in standards for organizational operations. Christ-centered ministries lock arms with profit and nonprofit organizations as diligent practitioners of best practices in every area of operation, especially in the leadership roles of the board chair and chief executive. The difference among these organizations begins with the motivation for their founding and the expectation for their outcomes.

Profit organizations are designed with a view to cost-benefit margins with the expectation for financial gain. Nonprofit organizations are motivated by social-benefit margins and the expectation for serving human need. Christ-centered ministries are founded for spiritual-benefit margins with the outcome of redemptive change. Once this baseline is achieved for under-standing the difference in the motivation and expectation for these organizations, we can go on to the specific question for this book: What then is the distinctive role of the board chair for the Christ-centered ministry?

The question is not answered by an overlay of spiritual jargon or a division between sacred and secular components. The integration of Christ-centered principles with the leadership standards of best practices in management is our mandate. The board chair of the Christ-centered ministry must be called of God to the position, exemplify Christ in qualifications, exercise Spirit-guided discernment in functions, and be accountable to God for performance. Our task now is to search out the full meaning of this mandate.

## 2

# CHOSEN BY GOD

How often have you heard a person talk about being called of God to serve as board chair? In most cases, we think of the position as the call of the board more than the call of God. The position itself is most unusual. While the standards of good practice for leadership are automatically expected of the board chair; seldom, if ever, is the person elected by competitive search, empowered for executive action, authorized to speak as an individual voice, or held accountable for performance. Sixty years of watching board leaders of Christ-centered ministries come and go from office tell us that we need to take another look at the board chair, its call, its identity, and its expectations.

## The Call of the Board

As the baseline for understanding the role of the chair, no one questions the fact that the person serves at the call of the board. The nature of the call, however, varies from board to board and organization to organization. Reflections from the past offer at least five different ways in which the board calls the chair.

**The Successor.** Most common in my experience is the chair who comes to the position through a laddered process. Starting as a member of the board, the person moves up the rungs of the ladder of position, first by chairing a board committee, next by being elected as one of the corporate officers, and then ascending to the vice-chair with the assumption that the chairmanship is next in line.

The system works, but it does not guarantee the quality of candidate needed to lead the board, especially in changing or controversial times. Emotion can take over this process. In the unwritten history of every Christ-centered ministry, there is a chapter telling the story of a member of the board who has climbed the ladder of hierarchy until reaching the level of his or her incompetence. Change is needed for the good of the ministry, but it comes not without inflicting wounds that may lead to bitterness and even resignation.

The crisis could be avoided by the selection of the chair according to criteria consistent with the expectations for board leadership, especially in changing times and critical moments.

**The Exemplar.** Close behind the Successor comes the Exemplar as board chair. By nature, boards of Christ-centered ministries nurture a seniority system for leadership. Individuals who persist in love and loyalty for the ministry over a long period of time are rewarded with leadership positions that may well include being elected as chair of the board. These persons stand above the process and defy attempts at term limits.

My experience with Exemplar chairs is positive. Even though they may not always be in sync with futuristic plans for the ministry, their loyalty usually overrides their doubts, and their love comes down on the side of hope.

Exemplar chairs are often filled by founders of the ministry. It is natural that the person who has the vision and passion to start the ministry continues in leadership after its successful growth requires an administrative organization with a governing board. The transition is not always successful.

I remember a "Mom and Pop" startup of a ministry related to world missions that was so successful that it quickly outdistanced its two-person operation. To go forward, a governing board, an experienced administrator, and a specialized staff had to be put into place. Even though the founder held the position as chair of the board, it quickly became evident that his gifts of entrepreneurial leadership did not match the demands for policy governance. Stress leading to conflict and ultimate separation cut adrift a creative spirit who could not make the adjustment to a structured system over which he did not have full control.

**The Rotator.** To avoid the potential conflicts of the Successor chair or the Exemplar chair, many organizations opt for the Rotator chair. As in the game of musical chairs, members of the board scurry for the open seat when their turn comes. The term of the Rotator chair is usually as short as a year or two. The idea is that the ministry can survive incompetence for a short period of time.

Sad moments come when a strong leader assumes the role and performs with skill but has to be replaced for the sake of the process. In such cases, the chief executive has to make the most of the time working with a competent chair and wait out the time of the weak leader.

The fault line of this system runs deep. Too much power is put into the hands of executive leaders, and too little continuity is provided for the development of the board itself. Worst of all, a relationship of verified trust between the board chair and the chief executive cannot be established in such a limited span of time.

**The Politician.** Oftentimes, board members of Christ-centered ministries are representatives of political units within the constituency. These units may be created by denominational conferences, religious preferences, geographical sections, stakeholder interests, or liberal and conservative factions. As might be expected, these groups can cluster and become cliques. When this happens, the purpose of the board is compromised, and its actions reflect special interests rather than collegial governance. In many cases, members are elected to the board not because of their qualifications but because of their affiliation.

A dysfunctional board is a natural outcome of a chair elected by special interest, an executive committee stacked with its members, and committee chairs who fall into line. In one of the institutions where I served, we had the fun of naming one of those segments "The Texas Mafia" because the chair, his successor, and key leaders of the board came from Texas. Because we could name it and laugh at it, we were able to able to keep it in balance and eventually meld it into a more diverse and representative board.

**The Dissenter.** Even Christ-centered ministries have tribal rebellions against the incumbent or pending leadership of the board that culminates in a change of the chair. The protest is usually along theological or philosophical lines.

An actual case illustrates the point. A board operating on the Successor model came to the time when the vice-chair waited in the wings to take over leadership. Alerts went out because the person's theology differed significantly from the historic position of the ministry, and the candidate's perception of the mission required a radical change. Parochial interests were awakened with alarm, and another board member was asked to be a candidate, breaking the Successor principle. When the Dissenter candidate was elected, the presumptive candidate resigned. One of the keenest minds was lost to the board.

This illustration underscores a point that needs to be made time and time again: the chair has a responsibility for the preserving the mission of the ministry through the succession of board leadership. While not pre-anointing or naming the successor, the role of the board chair includes identifying and developing potential leaders for the chair as well as committees. Integral to that responsibility is the evidence that potential leaders "own" the mission, as stated in official documents and articulated by the board chair. If this had been done in the Dissenter case cited above, a host of hurts would have been avoided.

Successor, Exemplar, Rotator, Politician, and Dissenter—each of these paths to the position as chair of the board is deficient in the criteria for leadership of the Christ-centered ministry. Like a roll of the dice, these office holders can be examples of Christian leadership at its best or at its worst.

We need to back up and start over with the primary qualification for the board chair. That qualification is none other than the call of God.

# The Call of God

Why the call of God upon the chair of the board? We cannot avoid the obvious answer. Without the call of God upon our board chair, we cannot make the claim for Christ-centered leadership. Without the call of God, we cannot expect the board chair to give the task highest priority of time, energy, and resources. Without the call of God, all of the high-sounding words about servanthood, stewardship, and sacrifice sound like the grating noise of a hollow gong.

It takes the call of God to hold integrity, cultivate relationships of trust, and remain humble. Loud and clear, we again hear Jesus calling us to follow Him: "The Son of Man did not come to be served, but to serve, and to give His life as a ransom for many" (Matt. 20:28). Servanthood characterized by stewardship with sacrifice is the call of God for the board chair of the Christ-centered ministry.

## Response to the Call

As always, the call of God requires a human response. The board chair who responds, "Here am I, send me" (Isa. 6:8) has to answer some critical questions:

1. Do I have the integrity, trust, and humility of a Christ-centered mind and spirit?

2. Do I have a Spirit-guided passion for the job?

3. Do I accept the limits of authority that can only be conferred by the full board?

4. Do I have respect for the chief executive?

5. Do I have the confidence of the full board?

6. Do I have the time for the task?

7. Do I have the patience for the process?

8. Do I have the gift for leading a messy but productive process?

9. Do I consider myself a good coach for the development of the chief executive and members of the board?

10. Do I accept the accountability that goes with the job?

## Proof in Practice

Here we stand. The chair for a Christ-centered ministry must be called of God as well as elected by the board. When the time comes for a board to elect a new chair, all business should stop while the members reflect in silence and ask that the Spirit of God might give them discernment in their selection. In the induction of the chair that follows, there should be the question, "Has God called you to this leadership position?" The prayer that follows should seal that call with the sacredness of the moment. If done in a consecration service for the board, its officers, and its members, the significance of the chair is communicated throughout the organization.

In the earlier months of my first presidency, I learned why the chair of the board should be in response to the call of God. We were in start-up mode for the development of a four-year Christian liberal arts college. Our plans far exceeded our resources. With some daring, we called in Tom Jones, President of Earlham College, a prominent liberal arts college in the

Quaker tradition, as our consultant. Rather than bringing a template for the college with him and talking about strategic planning, his first request was to meet with Hugh White, Chair of the Board. At the meeting, Dr. Jones pressed Mr. White to outline his commitments and give them priority. One by one, Mr. White cited his burgeoning business, his leadership of world missions for the denomination, his commitment to the local church, and his role as board chair for the fledging college. Then Mr. White stumbled as he tried to order them by priority. "Stop," the consultant said. "If you are the chair and this college is to succeed, you will have to make it your number-one priority, with everything else in second place." A strong message to be sure, but the chair took it seriously and gave his time, energy, and money to the college in its formative years.

While I as president get a lot of credit for building the four-year college, I can cite instance after instance when the commitment of the Hugh White and his wife, Edna, made the difference at turning points during those start-up years. One instance stands out. We came to an intersection in our planning when we had to have a new residence hall to keep pace with the required enrollment increase. Continuing accreditation hung in the balance. When our executive committee met to deal with the issue, Chairman White opened the meeting with one of his classic "little stories." He told about a pillow talk he'd had with his wife the night before. After thinking and praying about the crisis, together they came to a conclusion. The chair then announced, "My wife and I have decided that we want to give our money while we are alive so that we can have the joy of seeing it at work. We will build the residence hall." Even today, a bronze plaque in the lobby of the residence hall is a teaching moment for students and visitors alike. It reads:

## The Christ-centered Chair

Once we have heeded the call of God as our starting point, we can go forward and see the role of the board chair unfold in the transformative dimensions of leadership in the Christ-centered ministry. The term Christ-centered cannot slip off our tongue with ease. If we are who we say we are, it means that the mind of Jesus Christ is present in us and goes beyond the "highest dictates of natural reason and human conscience."[1] Therefore, every function and relationship in the tasks of the Christ-centered board chair will reflect the integration of His mind and spirit.

The Christ-centered board chair is a:

- **Missionary** – assuring that the policy-making role of the board is consistent with the God-given mission to meet a basic human and spiritual need;

- **Model** – exemplifying the integrity, trust, and humility of Christian leadership in a relational and collaborative setting with the board and its chief executive;

- **Mentor** – nurturing the development of the chief executive through a unique personal/professional/spiritual relationship of total trust;

- **Manager** – partnering with the chief executive to steward the time and task of the board through its committee structure and its working agenda to achieve the mission, realize the vision, and set the tone for the ministry;

- **Moderator** – cultivating a communal spirit for productive board interaction through engaged communication, diverse dialogue, consensus building, conflict resolution, and shared decision-making;

- **Mediator** – guiding the board through the threats of internal and external conflict into the opportunities for resolution, management, and transformation as witness of reconciliation in the Body of Christ;

- **Monitor** – assessing the performance of the board according to the principles of good governance, achievement of the God-given mission, and the personal/professional/spiritual growth of its members;

- **Master** – being alert for warning signs of action by board members or the board itself that deviate from the purpose or undercut the integrity of the Christ-centered ministry;

- **Maestro** – orchestrating the functions, relationships, and decisions of board governance into a harmonious whole that glorifies God.

Our question—"What is the distinctive role of the board chair for the Christ-centered ministry?"—is now answered. Incarnation continues in the identity of the board chair of the Christ-centered ministry as being is integrated with doing. With the character of "Christ in you" (Col. 1:27) enacted in the functions of effective leadership, the board chair is open and obedient to the call of God. Our purpose in writing, then, is to trace what it means for the board chair of the Christ-centered ministry to demonstrate the spirit of a Godly life while functioning according to the highest standards of leadership practice.

Forgive my penchant for a mnemonic listing. The names—Missionary, Model, Mentor, Manager, Moderator, Mediator, Monitor, Master, Maestro—fell naturally into place as the writing progressed and will guide us as we go forward. Stay with me as the story unfolds.

# PART II

## GOVERNANCE OF THE CHAIR

# 3

# MISSIONARY

*Assuring the policy-making role of the Board
consistent with the God-given mission to meet
a basic human and spiritual need."*

Does the title "Missionary" apply to the chair of the board of a
Christ-centered ministry? In our split-world stereotypes, we
tend to think of a missionary as a person whom God has called
to sacrifice all of the benefits of human achievements, serve in
an alien culture, and accept a lowly, risky position without
secular acclaim. Quite the opposite for the board chair of
Christ-centered ministry. Title, stature, power, and recognition
go with the job. Success is more common than sacrifice, service
is in a compatible community, and risk is almost nonexistent.

How then can we propose that the board chair be known as a
"Missionary? The answer is that the primary responsibility of
the chair is to lead the board as guardian of the mission for the
ministry. Without exception, when the responsibilities of the
board are spelled out in rank order, the preservation and
advancement of the chartered mission comes first.

There are good reasons for this mandate. The board represents continuity throughout the history of the organization. Chief executives come and go every four or five years, but members of the board overlap these times of administrative change. Furthermore, position descriptions for the recruitment of the chief executive invariably call for "visionary leadership" with the assumption that the mission will remain intact through and between tenures.

Even more important is the fact that the board is the legal owner of the organization and legally liable for the fulfillment of its chartered purpose. In others words, a board cannot delegate responsibility for the preservation and advancement of the chartered mission to the chief executive or anyone else. Even the farsighted and engaging vision of the chief executive for strategic planning in changing times must be honed against the whetstone of the primary mission. The chair is "first among equals" in responsibility for reminding the board that visionary ventures as well as routine policies and standard practices must pass the mission test.

Putting these thoughts together, we come to three responsibilities for the board chair as guardian of the mission. First, the board chair must take the lead to assure the *clarity* of the mission. Second, the board chair must assure the *consistency* of the mission. Third, the board chair must assure the *currency* of the mission. Let me speak to each point.

## Clarity of Mission

As first among equals, the chair of the board must assure the *clarity* of the mission. When we think about a Christ-centered ministry, we assume that the mission of the organization is clear, clean, and communicable for board members. Experience does not confirm that assumption. Surfing through the online mission statements of Christ-centered organizations leads to the conclusion that a many of these statements are mushy, muddled, and almost meaningless. A mix of the language of theology and management is used to give the mission statement credibility, but in fact the visitor to the website has to wonder how the mission connects to reality and motivates its followers.

In many cases, a mantra substitutes for the mission. Currently, almost every Christian ministry, including denominations, institutions, and independent movements, is claiming leadership development as the way for changing the world. From one perspective of our evangelical history, however, we are either victims or culprits in overemphasizing ever-changing schemes for ministries. In my lifetime, for instance, I can remember street corner meetings, mass rallies in stadiums, door-to-door missions, relational theology, church growth, political power, and church planting all having their day ahead of leadership development. Admittedly, I write with an edge of criticism, but not without confessing that I participated in all of those movements myself. Perhaps these thrusts for relevance are our Spirit-guided response to contemporary and changing needs, but behind them must be the clarity of mission as initially given in the Great Commission.

In my book *Power to Follow, Grace to Lead*, I devote a chapter to the statement of mission as vital to the strategy of any Christ-centered ministry.[2] Jesus leads the way with His first public sermon in Capernaum. Reaching back into the roots of Isaiah's prophecy, Jesus announces:

The Spirit of the Lord is on me, because He has anointed me to proclaim good news to the poor. He has sent me to proclaim freedom for the prisoners and recovery of sight for the blind, to set the oppressed free, to proclaim the year of the Lord's favor (Luke 4:18-19).

In a speech of sixty words that can be spoken in just thirty seconds, Jesus dares to make His mission public and hold Himself accountable for the outcomes. Delving deeper into Jesus's words, we see that all of the criteria that management consultants require a mission statement are fully met:

- Mandate: "The Spirit of the Lord is on me…"

- Motive: "He has anointed me…"

- Medium: "to preach…"

- Message: "good news…"

- Market: "The poor."

- Measure: "freedom for prisoners…sight for the blind…release for the oppressed…"

- Mood: "the year of the Lord's favor."

The board chair can use the following eight questions as a test for the clarity of our mission in the Christ-centered ministry:

1. Is our mission statement consistent with our vision?

2. Is our mission statement operational and measureable?

3. Does our mission statement identify our spiritual authority?

4. Does our mission statement specify the medium for our message?

5. Does our mission statement express the truth with grace?

6. Does our mission statement select the market for our ministry?

7. Does our mission statement include the goal of measureable change?

8. Does our mission statement carry the keynote of hope?

In a board meeting that I chaired, I used Jesus's mission statement as a devotional thought and then put out this challenge to our trustees: "Assume that you are at a conference and wearing a badge identifying you as a trustee of your ministry. You get on a high-rise elevator that will take sixty seconds to reach your floor. A stranger gets on with you, checks your badge, and asks, 'What is this all about?' You have sixty seconds to make your mission clear to a stranger. What would you say?"

It is no surprise to learn that most trustees came off like the blind men trying to identify an elephant. Bits and pieces of the mission were given, but almost everyone struggled to make a clear, clean, and communicable statement. This is why the board chair has to be the first one who can give the thirty-second elevator speech. When the chair welcomes the board members and makes an opening statement to set the text and tone for the meeting, a recitation of the elevator speech is in order.

## Consistency of Mission

During the board meeting itself, the chair may have to stop proceedings that are running off track and ask again, "Is this consistent with our mission?"

I have often spoken and written about the experience that led me to this question. While serving as president at Asbury Theological Seminary, my entrepreneurial impulses envisioned a retirement center for alumni and friends who held Wilmore, Kentucky, as their beloved spiritual home even though they had travelled to every corner of the earth in their ministerial callings. After confirming the need, exploring the options, and engaging leaders of the church and community, I enthusiastically presented my initial proposal to our board of trustees. The response was equally enthusiastic until the lone voice of a federal district judge from Houston, Texas, raised the question, "Is this consistent with our mission?" My train on a fast track came to a screeching halt. The trustees stopped and began to ask whether or not we would be diverting from our core mission of graduate theological education if we took on the ownership and management of a retirement center. When the discussion ended, the board chair had the sense of the meeting and concluded that we should look at other options for the retirement center that did not include direct involvement of the seminary because it could be a diversion from our primary mission. At the same time, the trustees affirmed their interest in the vision, pledged their support for the project by having a liaison member as part of future planning, and agreed to consider selling prime seminary land for the retirement campus. The good news is that church and civic leaders from the local community and the regional area rallied to the project and built the magnificent senior center, appropriately named "Wesley Village."

Is it consistent with our mission? This question must be asked time and time again because every board is tempted to take on programs that cause drift or distortion of the mission. In consultation with boards of Christ-centered ministries, I have seen the adoption of programs that promised to be cash cows for meeting desperate financial needs—but at the price of losing integrity in the mission. I have also seen boards turn a blind eye and a deaf ear to internal programs that are seriously out of balance with the mission but are presumably untouchable because of popularity or personality. Sadder yet, I have seen Christ-centered ministries sell their souls for the pottage of governmental funds. If the board chairs had asked the trustees or directors of these ministries to take the mission test, they would have had to ride roughshod over good judgment to approve such programs.

## Currency of Mission

Rapidly changing and growing programs of ministry present a special challenge to the integrity of mission. Again, in my online survey of mission statements in Christ-centered ministries, I frequently find instances where new programs outrun the mission statement. The same can be said about fast-growing programs where sheer numbers will skew the working balance of the original mission.

Returning to the statement of Jesus in his first public sermon at Capernaum, we see in the Gospel of Mark the progressive unfolding of his mission. The first half of the Gospel is given to the story of Jesus as servant for the physical, emotional, and spiritual needs of His hearers. Through this ministry He reveals Himself to His disciples. Peter speaks for the Twelve when he answers Jesus's question "Who do you say that I am?" by confessing, "You are the Messiah" (Mark 8:29).

From that peak of understanding, Jesus takes them to the next chapter of His mission: "He then began to teach them that He must suffer many things and be rejected by the elder, chief priests and teachers of the law, and he must be killed and after three days rise again." (Mark 8:31) This is more than the disciples can comprehend or absorb. When Peter rebukes Him for a radical pronouncement, Jesus counters with the strong words, "Get behind me, Satan. You do not have in mind the concerns of God, but merely human concerns" (Mark 8:33). Jesus has now made the transition from Christ the servant to Christ the suffering servant. From then on, He continues to add details to the reality of His suffering, but His core mission never changes. Through the ministry of His life, He brings freedom from suffering; through the ministry of His death, He brings freedom from sin.

The mission statement of the Christ-centered ministry will also be subject to refinement and change, but the core of its calling must remain intact. I recall conversations with the board of trustees about the introduction of graduate studies in a four-year Christian liberal arts college and changing the name from "College" to "University." In each case, healthy debate followed before the policy decision was made. Christ-centered ministries must never let their mission statement deter a legitimate response to changing needs or let new opportunities overrun their mission statement.

Who will be the guardian for the mission of the Christ-centered ministry if not the board chair? Yes, we expect the chief executive to develop a vision and strategy consistent with the mission. Yes, we expect the board to adopt policies and practices that preserve and advance the mission. Yes, we expect that the core mission can be lived out in chapters of response to changing need. But again, experience shows that someone needs to ride point on the assignment. Who better than the chair of the board? The title of "Missionary" is a position of highest honor.

# MODEL

*Exemplifying the integrity, trust and humility
of Christ-centered leadership
in a relational and collaborative setting
with the Board and the Chief Executive.*

Why the call of God upon the chair of the board? Go back to
the three qualifications of integrity, trust, and humility that
are on the bridge between the caliber of personal character
and the transformational impact of the mind and spirit of
Jesus Christ. How does such transformation take place? The
process is no secret.: (1) a Christian leader aligns his will with
the will of God, wherever that may lead; (2) an unfulfilled
ministry need appears as a challenge; (3) the prompting of
the Holy Spirit connects the leader's gift with the unmet
need; and (4) the board connects the two in a vote of
confirmation.

For the candidate, submission to the will of God, the counsel
of others, and the confirmation of the election seal the call.
A board chair comes to the position called by the choice of
God and confirmed by the election of the board.

# Christ-centered Integrity

Scripture confirms the call of God in practical terms. As noted earlier, in the standard of good practices the board chair of any organization is expected to lead with integrity. At the root of the word's meaning is *completeness* or *wholeness*. Integrity, then, is a natural step toward the transforming truth "In [Christ], all things hold together" (Col. 1:17). Through Him and Him alone can we claim the name "Christ-centered." Whether in the ethics of the individual or the ethos of the organization, everything is Christ-centric, and once again the board chair is called to be the example as first among equals.

Truth-telling is the test of integrity in leadership. A board chair is put to this test on a regular basis and with multiple constituencies. The truth of good and bad news must be told to the board, chief executive, staff, constituencies, and the general public. How it is told in a Christ-centered context will determine whether or not the chair has integrity. To assume that the truth must always be told bald-faced with naked facts fails to recognize the skill of diplomacy and the gift of discernment required of a board chair. When I asked Oregon Senator Mark Hatfield how he retained his impeccable integrity as a Christian and a politician, he answered, "You can compromise on timing, wording, and procedure, but never on principle."

As a board chair, I tried to put the senator's wisdom into practice when communicating the truth about volatile issues. The time for truth-telling can vary from the urgent to the long term, wording can be crafted to avoid inflammatory phrases, and procedure can be adjusted to deal with the issue in different ways. In none of these cases, however, can the principle of truth be compromised at the cost of integrity for the Christ-centered ministry or validity for its Christian witness.

Hatfield's working principle especially applies in a time when truth is being spun to deceive the public and manipulate its opinion. Rather than whining over this reality, leaders of Christ-centered ministries, beginning with the board chair, have an opportunity to make integrity the hallmark of our witness.

Integrity comes not from human effort or good conscience but from the saving grace of "Christ in us" (Col. 1:27) and the sanctifying grace of His Holy Spirit working within us. Our integrity is not our own. In ourselves we have no claim on righteousness. Only through the transforming mind of Christ can we claim the qualities of character revealed in Philippians 4:8:

> Finally, brothers and sisters, whatever is true, whatever is noble, whatever is right, whatever is pure, whatever is lovely, whatever is admirable—if anything is excellent or praiseworthy—think about such things.

Scripture sets the highest standard of excellence for the personal integrity and public credibility of the board chair in the Christ-centered ministry. Without integrity, nothing else counts.

## Christ-centered Trust

Step up to the expectation that a board chair will develop relationships of trust that transcend the boundaries of human interaction. Dan Busby, President of the Evangelical Council for Financial Accountability, leads 3,000 Christ-centered ministries in the pursuit of public trust by a process of self-regulation.

Busby sums up his experience in a book entitled *TRUST, The Firm Foundation for Kingdom Fruitfulness*, which he sees as the permeating principle engaging, convicting, and empowering every aspect of the Christ-centered ministry.[3]

Trust is such a fragile bond in human relationships. By contractual agreement, trust can be a legal arrangement among potential adversaries. In international affairs, trust can be a tenuous pact that remains suspicious without verification. In the public sphere, we are shocked to learn how far the level of trust has fallen for established authorities in government, business, and even religion. The board chair of any organization has to counter these negative forces by fostering working relationships of goodwill and common purpose.

As I learned early in my experience as a board chair, trust comes with consistency. In my acceptance of the role, I pledged to the board, "I will do exactly as I say I will do, and if I change my mind, you will be the first to know." Even then, we know that trust can be broken by others who misunderstand us or by ourselves when we are inconsistent.

What then is the difference in the trust relationship of a board chair functioning at the highest level of consistency and the Christ-centered leader working with transformational resources? Scripture leads us to the answer:

> This, then, is how you ought to regard us: as servants of Christ and as those entrusted with the mysteries God has revealed. Now it is required that those who have been given a trust must prove faithful (I Cor. 4:1-2).

Once again, we bow before eternal truth. Trust is earned, in both personal and public relationships, by being consistent servants of Christ and faithful stewards of the Word. This is the Christ-centric trust undergirding the board chair in establishing and maintaining relationships with the board, the chief executive, and all of the other stakeholders.

## Christ-centered Humility

Integrity and trust are like a two-legged stool for board leadership. They will not stand without humility. As with all leadership positions, the board chair is susceptible to the temptations of arrogance, dominance, and manipulation. Sad to say, each of us has seen this happen. We can recall board chairs that take the role for their own aggrandizement; others have worked behind the scenes to compete with the chief executive officer; and still others have refused to be accountable for their actions.

Even for the board chair of a Christ-centered ministry, the temptation persists. Without humility, all of the pretty words about servanthood, stewardship, and sacrifice sound like self-serving chatter. It takes the call of God to hold integrity, cultivate the relationships of trust that the role requires, and remain humble. Loud and clear, the scripture confronts us with the challenge to have the mind of Christ in our leadership:

> Do nothing out of selfish ambition or vain conceit. Rather, in humility value others above yourselves, not looking to your own interests but each of you to the interests of the others (Phil. 2:3-4).

If we were to put an all-embracing caveat over the role of the board of the Christ-centered ministry, this would be it. Leadership with integrity, stewardship with trust, and servanthood with humility are the sum and substance of the call of God upon the board chair of the Christ-centered ministry.

First and foremost; integrity, trust, and humility are qualities of organizational character that come down from the top. They do not bubble up from within the organization but come directly from the model of its leaders. Moreover, these qualities have the power of permeation. Like isotopes in the blood stream, once integrity, trust, and humility are injected into the arteries of the organization, every cell is affected.

Conversely, the absence of these qualities in the board chair as first among equals will cause the contamination of dishonesty, suspicion, and arrogance throughout the system. A dysfunctional board is just the beginning of the price to be paid when the chair is not the model of integrity, trust, and humility. But when these virtues of Christ-centered character are consciously and unconsciously present in the life and leadership of the chair, every ensuing function of his or her task takes on the promise of an effective organization with a credible witness.

# 5

# MENTOR

*Nurturing the development of the Chief Executive
and members of the Board through a unique
personal/professional/spiritual relationship.*

If I were asked to identify the fulcrum point upon which the
Christ-centered ministry balances to change the world, my
answer would be instant and unequivocal. The relationship
between the board chair and the chief executive sets the text
and tone for the whole organization. I speak from experience.
From both sides of equation, having been a chief executive
and a board chair, I have known compatibility, conflict,
compromise, and conciliation in the relationship. Looking back
on this personal history, I see what it means to have a Christ-
centered relationship between the board chair and chief
executive in the Christ-centered ministries.

## Covenant Colleague

Unconditional trust has already been identified as the defining
factor in all relationships in the Christ-centered ministries.
Now it comes to the critical point of focus in the relationship
between the board chair and the chief executive. It begins with

sharing a common faith. Because board chairs and chief executives are usually strong-minded people with a record of success, there will be differences of opinion that need to be aired, but not in a public setting where disagreement can be misinterpreted as a breach in top leadership that ripples through the system.

The board chair–chief executive relationship can be likened to a husband and wife who are responsible for discipline of their children. Wisdom says that the couple should go into the bedroom, resolve their differences, and come back with a unified decision for consistency in discipline. Otherwise, the children have no clear line of demarcation for the development of character. Likewise, in their regular and private meetings, the board chair and chief executive should be fully honest with each other about their differences and work through them to a unified and consistent position for presentation to the board.

There will be times when the differences appear to be irreconcilable. If and when that time comes, the board chair and chief executive must fall back upon their common faith in Jesus Christ, agree to disagree, and decide what is best for the good of the ministry. As rare as these occasions may be, they represent a covenant of trust between Christians that needs to be cultivated as part of our witness.

A covenantal trust often takes the board chair and the chief executive into the realm of confidentiality. How many chief executives can confess their doubts and fears to their board chairs? How many chairs can reveal the underground questions from the board about the effectiveness of the chief executive?

Lurking just beneath the surface of the board chair–chief executive relationship is the specter of the boss-employee connection. True, the board authorizes its chair to negotiate the terms for hiring the chief executive, assure the health and well-being of its leader, and announce the bad news if the chief executive is fired. The delicacy of this relationship reinforces the need for total trust between the board chair and the chief executive.

For me personally, I confess that as a chief executive, I had a distorted view of authority that caused me to keep my doubts and fears to myself. I dared not tell the chairs with whom I worked about my anxious moments, my spiritual conflicts, or my habit of looking at the announcements of presidential openings with a desire to flee. Consequently, regular meetings with the board chair centered upon gains rather than losses, promises rather than threats, and impersonal issues rather than personal concerns. We survived, but not without sacrificing the confidentiality of our covenant by over-emphasizing good news and downplaying negative issues. Out of this experience, I concluded that I needed a confidant for personal and spiritual well-being who had no vested interest in the institution where I served. Admittedly, the faith that the board chair and I held in common should have given the trust upon which confidentiality is based, but I suspect that I am not alone.

Sooner or later, the acid test will come with a moral or ethical crisis that requires the highest level of Christ-centered trust between the chair and the chief executive. Confidentiality may well be the latent growth factor in the board chair and chief executive relationship.

# Strategic Partner

Throughout my career I needed the wisdom check of a board chair who understood strategic planning and the multitude of issues that swirled around its implementation. The tendency is to leave strategic planning to the experts, with the board giving its rubber stamp. When this happens, the board chair–chief executive relationship is relegated to the lower level of tactical concerns, where the temptation is to micromanage.

If, however, the task description for the board chair gives high priority to a strategic partnership with the chief executive, the focus shifts to critical issues of planning directly connected with policy. Again, the chair is called to be first among equals of board members and the one who is immersed in the strategic planning process. This means the chair's interaction with the chief executive is a genuine partnership in which major issues are discussed, alternatives are considered, and resolutions are proposed.

Visionary and entrepreneurial chief executives are particularly in need of the checks and balances of an informed chair who serves as a sounding board for creative ideas and out-of-the-box proposals. In fact, consider the regular meetings of the chair and chief executive as a "mini think tank" where ideas and issues are presented, processed, and proposed for resolution prior to board meetings.

Together, the chair and chief executive should plan the agenda for their regular sessions as carefully as they prepare for the meeting of the full board. Priorities for strategic planning and policy come first. Assuming a strategic plan is in place, the session should be centered on the questions, "Is our focus on priorities?" "Is the plan on schedule?" and "What can we show as results?" Everything in these sessions points to the full board meeting, when the chair and chief executive stand together on proposals for strategy and policy that are worthy of the business of the board.

There is no substitute for efficacy, efficiency, and effectiveness in the strategic partnership of the board chair and chief executive. When this relationship exists, it translates into board sessions where every member joins the partnership in the vital work of strategic planning related to consistent policies and collegial decisions.

## Developmental Coach

A board that elects a chief executive, breathes a sigh of relief, and infers that the chief executive is on his or her own from now on is remiss in its responsibility. Even the most gifted chief executive has room to grow, and the board is obligated to invest in that growth.

Once again, enter the board chair. A Christ-centered board in particular cannot default from its responsibility to grow its chief executive officer. While all of the board members must be vitally concerned about leadership development for its executive leader, it is the chair, in close relationship with the chief executive, who serves as coach for the process.

As a complement to the strategic plan, the chief executive sets long-term, mid-term, and short-term goals for his or her leadership. These goals need the checks and balances of the board chair–chief executive relationship.

As chair, I worked with the chief executive on the following processes:

- Each year, our chief executive formulated personal, professional, and spiritual goals as a plan for executive action.

- Together, we reviewed and refined these goals so that we were in full agreement before I presented them to the board for final discussion and general agreement.

- The chief executive chose the time and place to present these annual goals to the staff and the constituency in a "State of the Ministry" address.

- Later, at one of our midyear meetings, I brought these goals back to see how the chief executive was progressing, and together we made any necessary corrections.

- At the close of the year, we returned to an assessment of chief executive performance against the goals.

- In an executive session of the board without the chief executive, I as chair summarized the assessment and asked for affirmative recommendations for improving chief executive performance and providing resources to back them up.

- Afterward, I reported back to the chief executive to make the recommendations part of a personal/professional/spiritual growth plan on which we all agreed. From there, the cycle started over again.

The growth plan for the chief executive also has merit as a governance plan for the board as well. As part of agenda planning for the year, the board could reserve time in its sessions for initial goal-setting, midcourse correction, and final assessment of its governing responsibility. While leading the process, the chair could also suggest that individual board members work through the same process as a plan for personal growth and improved governance. It is certainly worth a try.

## Wellness Facilitator

By authorization of the board, the chair has the privilege of assuring the health and well-being of the chief executive. *Wellness* in the sense of wholeness leads us directly into the truth that Christ-centered well-being makes whole our physical, psychological, and spiritual well-being. Much more is involved than a salary guaranteeing sufficient economic freedom to do the job. At the time of the election of the chief executive, it is the chair who negotiates the contractual agreement with the candidate.

Having been the chief executive of three Christ-centered institutions who never had a written contract, I agree with the need for such an agreement. However, I still find it awkward for a Christ-centered ministry. In my case, the salary was set and the benefits were standard. For better or worse, so much more is required today. Compensation is spelled out in details of salary, health insurance, retirement plans, housing, automobile, expense accounts, vacation, and even severance provisions. All well and good, but what is the effect of a Christ-centered mindset?

Front and center, compensation for the chief executive should be based upon need; not upon wants, wishes, or competitive status. Furthermore, those needs should be basic to a reasonable level of economic security for the chief executive and family in the present and the future.

The pressure, of course, is on competitive dollars and secular status. Both as a chief executive and a board chair, I resisted the race to the top by insisting that executive compensation stay within range of administrative and staff compensation in the organization. One time, I had to deal with the opposite problem. A chief executive who was independently wealthy took a minimal salary and ended up depressing the compensation system for all other employees. As a consultant, I also had to deal with the board chair who made a fortune in the secular world but felt that poverty and purity went hand in hand in Christian ministry.

Compensation of the chief executive in the Christ-centered ministry is integral to our witness in the world. Almost every scandal that has plagued evangelical Christianity in recent history has involved fraud and financial corruption in the compensation package of the chief executive. Both responsibility and opportunity for the well-being of the chief executive is given to the chair by the board. In the Christ-centered context, well-being is meeting the financial needs of the chief executive so that he or she is free to take on the strenuous task of leadership while being protected from the competitive pressures that can ruin our Christian witness.

# Assessment Coordinator

Accountability weighs heavy in the cycle of chief executive performance and growth. Even though a governance committee or an outside consultant may be involved in the assessment of the chief executive, coordination of the process rests with the board chair. As noted earlier, the annual leadership cycle for the chief executive involves an informal assessment, with the chair communicating the results in an executive session with the full board.

Every three to five years, the process needs to be formalized in a 360-degree review, usually conducted by an outside consultant. In this case, the criteria for review go back to the personal, professional, and spiritual qualifications on which the chief executive was elected as well as the outcomes expected from his/her leadership.

Here again, spiritual growth and maturity enter the equation in the Christ-centered ministry. The board chair in particular must assure that the spiritual dimensions are included in the assessment because communication of the results to the chief executive and the board go with the position. It takes spiritual growth to know spiritual growth, and it takes spiritual maturity to know spiritual maturity. To be a mentor with the mind of Christ, the board chair needs to be a model with the spirit of Christ as well as a manager who gets things done.

# 6

# MANAGER

*Partnering with the Chief Executive to steward the time
and task of the Board through its policy, composition,
structure, and agenda to achieve the mission for the
Christ-centered ministry.*

The board chair dances on a razor's edge between executive
and managerial leadership. Technically, the board chair is not
an executive because the position is located outside a chain
of command with authority for implementing policy and
accountability for achieving the plan. At the same time, the
chair is a manager responsible for stewarding the resources of
policy, people, and procedures that assure an effective board in
support of executive action. Summed up in a sentence, the chair
manages the board, and the chief executive officer manages the
organization.

The standard functions of the board chair are well known—
presiding at meetings of the board and its executive committee;
collaborating with the chief executive in the recruiting,
orientation, development, and assessment of board members;
exercising authority from the board for legal matters and public

communication; making appointments for board committees, commissions, and task forces; serving ex officio on all board committees, commissions, and task forces; and planning the working agenda with the chief executive for all board and executive committee meetings.

In a Christ-centered organization, it is expected that the board chair brings the mind of Christ to the discernment of direction and the spirit of Christ to leading the way. Out of these standard functions, then, three stand out as deserving special attention by the board chair of a Christ-centered ministry: developing the board, planning the agenda, and presiding over the meetings.

## Developing the Board

If we're being honest, we must admit that the recruitment, orientation, development, and assessment of board members is usually a casual process and a second-level priority for the chair. However, in the Christ-centered and mission-driven organization, these factors should be identified and followed as first-line responsibilities.

**Recruitment.** If you ask the chair of any organization about the standards required for the recruitment of board members, the traditional reply will be "work, wealth, and wisdom," with an emphasis upon wealth. In Christ-centered ministries, the standard needs to be elevated to "character, conviction, and compulsion," with an emphasis upon character. Potential members will have the character of Christ, the conviction of the Word, and the compulsion of God's call to serve in this particular ministry.

Having established those ground rules, the chair and chief executive will work together to assure representative diversity in the composition of the board. Age, race, and gender apply at this point. Also, representation from supporting constituencies must be considered.

But these criteria cannot override the fundamental guideline for recruiting board members. Competence to match the needs of the mission and vision for the organization, as spelled out in the strategic plan, should have highest priority for the board chair and chief executive when they recruit future board members.

This process begins with identifying the competencies inferred in the strategic plan that need to be matched by the knowledge, experience, and wisdom of board members. Currently, the tendency is to start with the search for financial experts whose wealth confirms their success. Nothing is wrong with this if the baseline requirements for a Christ-centered ministry are met. Caution is in order. Because of the ever-present financial pressures on Christ-centered ministries, the board and executive committee can be dominated by members with financial expertise or success. To realize the comprehensive goals of the strategic plan, a wider range of knowledge, experience, and wisdom is needed. Persons with credentials and experience in legal matters, theological issues, market techniques, media communication, educational programming, human resource development, political affairs, and international relations are all examples of pending needs. In planning for the identification and recruitment of board members, the chair and chief executive should determine the competencies needed to complement the existing level of expertise on the board.

This plan may be frustrated by the election of board members from constituencies that value the independence of their vote. I faced this situation in two of my presidencies in church-related universities. As I observed the process of election in these constituencies, I noted that the agenda item for election of members to our board often came after all of the choice positions were gone, so that the decision became a sentimental plum for senior members or compensation for a lost election bid. On more than one occasion, competence had nothing to do with the election. In fact, I remember contests where the person of choice directly opposed the direction of the school. Finally, after an inventory of our board composition and in agreement with the chair, we dared to prepare a list of competencies needed on our board in support of our strategic plan. When I shared that list with the leadership of our constituent conferences, I was surprised by the reception. The leaders expressed their gratitude for this help and worked actively to improve the quality of representation on the board.

**Orientation.** The chair, in partnership with the chief executive, has to take the lead in the orientation of new board members. This expectation can be a mixed bag. Orientation for new board members in Christ-centered ministries is usually casual if it happens at all. We can understand how close and longtime relationships between current and potential board members seem to make the process unnecessary. We can also understand how much orientation seems pointless for experienced and successful leaders in the church or corporate communities. Our assumptions are wrong.

No one comes to the position of a board member with prior preparation to serve. Even if the candidate has board experience in both secular and religious organizations, future effectiveness depends upon an in-depth understanding of the specific mission, targeted vision, and strategic plan of the Christ-centered ministry. I confess that I took full charge of board recruiting in my early presidencies and assumed that the candidates I had proposed were already well-versed in boardsmanship. Not until I became a board chair did I realize how essential orientation is to the board developmental process.

Orientation is complementary to recruitment according to competencies needed for implementing the strategic plan. New members to the board, no matter how spiritual, successful, or familiar, must learn and accept the mission, vision, and strategic plan as well as the policy and practices of the Christ-centered ministry.

Orientation is the process of introducing a new board member to the roots and shoots of the Christ-centered ministry. The roots are grounded in the rich soil of history, and the shoots take wing in the vast sky of vision. No one can serve effectively as a board member of the Christ-centered ministry who does not identify with these roots and embrace these shoots.

A packet sent to the incoming board member prior to the orientation session should always include information about the history, theology, and mission of the ministry as well as official documents, such as the charter, bylaws, policy manual, strategic plan, and copies of recent board minutes. In the orientation session, the chair and chief executive will want to highlight aspects of these documents as the basis for discussion with the inductees. Special attention needs to be given to drawing the distinction of the Christ-centered ministry and defining the cutting edge of the purpose to which the organization is dedicated. A personalized testimony from the chair in answer to the question, "What does our Christ-centered ministry mean to me?" is a most effective way to get the message across.

Orientation is the time when the chair deals directly with the expectation that the board member will participate in fundraising, more delicately called resource development, both in giving and asking. As chair, I did not hesitate to ask that 100 percent of the board make annual gifts to the ministry. Good reason backed up my request. As chief executive, I had learned that the first question of potential donors to the organization, whether foundation directors or individual prospects, was to ask, "What does the board give?" I found that the questioners were not just interested in the amount but in the level of participation. In fact, they understood the limits of resources among board members in fields of ministry and service but expected that full commitment meant full participation.

To reinforce this expectation for 100 percent annual giving was just the beginning. I went on to apply the principles of giving that I had learned from my fundraising experience with United Way. We worked with a graduated scale of giving:

- Give once (i.e., starter gift)

- Give regularly (i.e., payroll deduction)

- Give more (i.e., major gift)

- Give long-term (i.e., estate gift)

Using this scale, I upgraded the expectation for investment in the mission of the ministry by saying that board members had to lead the way. Then, I went the final step in the responsibility of the individual board member for fundraising by asking for a commitment from them to make personal contacts throughout their network of friends and associates on behalf of the Christ-centered ministry. Reaching back to my chief executive experience, I said that one of the most effective approaches to fundraising was have the chief executive and a board member go together to ask for a gift from one of the board member's contacts. I wish that I could report success in the implementation of this ambitious plan. I cannot.

As strange as it seems, we always had to make extra appeals to get 100 percent giving from the board. Even though I tried to set the example as chair in accompanying the chief executive on fundraising contacts, the response of board members was minimal. Experience says that this weakness in board commitment is not an exception for Christ-centered organizations. Even when the chair leads the way, passive resistance tends to rule.

The end goal of orientation is to make clear the expectations for a board member. Even though these expectations may be written in official documents, reinforcement is needed so that the trustee or director cannot be surprised by hidden expectations. Matters such as reading information sent out in advance of the board meeting, attendance in committee and general sessions, thoughtful and prayerful engagement in discussion, and participation in fundraising may seem obvious to us, but the fact of experience speaks otherwise. Not only in orientation, but from time to time in regular sessions, the chair has the responsibility for reminding the board of these expectations.

## Planning the Agenda

If asked to name the leadership tools available to the board chair, the usual answer would include presiding at board meetings; appointing the chairs and members of standing committees, commissions, and task forces; and serving as ex officio member of all committees, commissions, and task forces. A more subtle, but powerful, tool is the agenda for these meetings. Second only to the interpersonal relationship of trust, collaborative agenda-making by the board chair and chief executive is the fulcrum for their leverage as leaders.

Early on, I learned the power of this tool. A hit-and-miss approach to board business is an indicator of inefficiency and a promulgator of discontent. Board members are volunteers who cannot afford wasted time and leaders in their own spheres who will quickly become disquieted by undisciplined board sessions. Consequently, the board chair and chief executive should put a premium upon preparation of the agenda for the board, executive committee, and standing committees.

Experience has taught me, both as a chair and a chief executive, to prepare an agenda for board meetings based on the following working principles. First, the content for the agenda comes primarily from the issues, recommendations, and resolutions proposed by the chief executive with the refinement and concurrence of the board chair. No one questions the fact that the chief executive is the manager of the organization and held responsible for its health and welfare. So out of the crucible of executive action come the issues that the board needs to address and the recommendations that need to be considered for approval, revision, or rejection according to board policy. The chief executive's "State of the Ministry" address becomes the core of the agenda for the board meeting. While board members are invited to submit items for the agenda with the assurance of consideration, they should not override the presentation of the chief executive unless they involve issues that threaten the integrity of the ministry.

Second, the welcome of the chair at the opening of the meeting should be a "State of the Board" address for the purpose of setting the text and the tone for the meeting. A gracious, personalized welcome is certainly in order, but the chair misses a grand opportunity for leadership if the opening words do not highlight the goals, expectations, and potential outcomes for the meeting. Like a one-stringed banjo player, the chair will always sound the note reminding the members that the board's role is policy, not execution. This is the best way for the chair to send the signal of support for the chief executive and pave the way for implementing policy in executive recommendations. It is also the opportune moment for the chair to establish an interactive climate for the forthcoming sessions by inviting board members to propose additional items for the agenda. In response, the chair should acknowledge each of these items and indicate that they will be processed for inclusion under "Other Business" or referred to the executive committee for future consideration.

Third, the agenda should be planned to match the most salient items with the time, energy, and alertness of the board. It is no secret that board meetings can become boring and attention can be lost. Part of the problem is the natural cycle of the day.

Board members are most alert in the morning sessions and least alert right after lunch. Good planning for the agenda captures the best of those hours by providing adequate time for thorough discussion of the most significant items. Pacing of the agenda is equally important. Along with guiding the flow of balancing controversial issues with the unanimous support of a consent agenda, the chair leads by sensing the need for the white space of coffee and bathroom breaks, pauses for prayer before casting votes, and takes time for good reports from the staff or constituents on the impact of the ministry. To counter the inevitable temptation for board members to leave early, a trick of the chair is to schedule an item at the end of the agenda that no one wants to miss.

Fourth, as the final item on the agenda, the chair should close the loop with a statement assessing the effectiveness of the board session. Based on the chair's opening remarks during the "State of the Board," the criteria for assessment are readymade. The chair can state the goals accomplished, the issues still pending, and the work yet to be done.

Equally important, this is the time to speak frankly about the tone of the meeting and to appeal for the mind and spirit of Christ as the quality that defines the character of the board. Again, this is an opportune moment to engage the board members in the assessment process. For instance, the chair can invite board members to respond to the question, "How can we improve our effectiveness as a Christ-centered board?" The question invites constructive suggestions, increases self-awareness, and encourages self-assessment as a continuing expectation for the board.

A closing prayer led by the chair offers thanks for God's presence, asks for the guidance of the Holy Spirit as the chief executive implements board actions, and commits all of the members into His care during the time that they will be apart.

# MODERATOR

*Cultivating a communal spirit for productive
Board interaction through engaged communication,
diverse dialogue, consensus building,
and shared decision-making.*

What is the image of a board chair that comes to mind? Most likely, it will be the picture of a dignified and authoritative person presiding at the meeting of a corporate board and leading its members toward interactive and informed decisions. Behind the scenes, however, is a person who brings the gifts and skills of a confident leader, a masterful moderator, a knowledgeable parliamentarian, a sagacious diplomat, and a decisive closer. Add the dimensions of the Spirit-guided life for the Christ-centered chair, and we have a level of leadership that is far more than just the power of the gavel. No chair meets the ideal, but every chair has the potential to grow into the skills of presiding at board meetings with the gift of grace.

## Focusing on Policy

In a very real sense, the chair is the gatekeeper for a policy-making board. Slippage comes from every side. Board members want to micromanage, the chief executive wants to macro-manage, and staff members want to pick and chose among these alternatives. Years ago, John Carver introduced us to "Ends Results" policies that advance the mission and benefit the persons whom it serves.[4] An example is a policy that calls for a balanced budget on an annual basis. End results policies are brief, clear, comprehensive, and lead to three questions that the chair will ask again and again during board discussions:

- "Do we have a policy in this area?"

- "If so, is the proposal consistent with the policy?"

- "If not, do we need to prepare a policy to guide us now and in the future?"

Like the focus of a laser beam, these questions will put the board back on track.

Carver also armed us with "Executive Limitations," policies that draw boundaries for the delegated authority of the chief executive.[5] For the Christ-centered ministry, these policies are directly related to Biblical revelation. In the Garden of Eden, God gave Adam and Eve the full range of freedom to follow His commands and fulfill His promises. The only exception was the tree of life with its knowledge of good and evil, which God reserved for Himself. In effect, God gave Adam and Eve a policy of executive limitation, saying, "Go until I say stop." He did not say, "Stop until I say go."

The same confidence should be expressed in Christ-centered leadership. In its policy, the board plants the tree of life and tells its chief executive officer, "Go until we stay stop." The stopping point would be a proposal that is outside the range of end results policies, such as presenting an unbalanced budget. By following this plan, entrepreneurial freedom for the chief executive is assured and policy-making authority for the board is confirmed.

## Staffing the Structure

Policy cannot be enacted without people. Among the weighty responsibilities of the board chair is the appointment of standing committee chairs and committee membership. The task is not just a lottery pick or an award of rotation. In order to be gatekeeper for policy and guiding hand for the agenda, the chair must appoint people to committee positions according to the same criteria as when recruiting members for the board.

Consistent with the name of standing committee—such as finance, human resources, program development, marketing, or governance—the best minds and most representative members must be appointed from the board in each of these areas. Most important, however, is the naming of the committee chair. Here, the chair needs to have an eye for potential as well as proven leaders among board members. Criteria for leadership of committees must be the same as the qualifications for the board chair itself, even though the skills and gifts may still be in the making.

Prior to every session, the board chair will convene the committee chairs in order to assure they are in sync with the plan of the chair and chief executive, as evident in the agenda for the full board meeting. The board chair wants to get across four messages at these meetings:

- First, committee reports, discussions, and recommendations must be related to policy implementation and development.

- Second, the agenda for the committees must have its own priorities for dealing with policy-related items, providing adequate time for discussion, and bringing to the full board its position or motions on the major matters under consideration.

- Third, the committee chairs must avoid the temptation to turn the committee sessions into mini board meetings for the staff. While reports from the staff are needed for the committee to get a sense of the issues the staff faces and to encourage them in their work, unless the committee chair disciplines the time, reporting will take over the meeting. It is up to the chair to keep committee work focused on policy matters, just as the board chair does in full board sessions.

- Fourth, standing committees must be cautioned against making decisions or presenting proposals that deviate from the direction of the mission and vision as detailed in the strategic plan or in the chief executive's proposals for implementing that plan. This does not limit the committee from bringing new and relevant issues to the board for discussion and referral, but they must not undercut the chief executive's plan unless it is a contest of policy itself.

The leadership of the committee chair is judged effectively when the report of the committee to the board provides in-depth understanding along with wise judgment for dealing with the policy issues related to a specific charge; for example, human resources, advancement, finance. A forward-thinking chair will also see the position of committee chair as training ground for succession in board leadership. Discernment is a gift of the Holy Spirit that comes with spiritual maturity. It may well be the gift that defines Christ-centered leadership. If so, it is a gift that is given by grace and grows by experience. Early on, the presence or absence of this gift can be detected. Perceptive board chairs who have succession in mind will be on high alert for spotting this gift, especially among younger board members.

## Managing the Process

The board chair of the Christ-centered organization is called to be a student of human behavior in both personal and inter-personal dimensions. The dynamics of group process serve as our case in point. As always, Jesus serves as our example. Several times during His ministry, He put brakes on the speed of His ministry by saying, "My hour has not yet come" (John 2:4). In other instances, He put the white space of rest and reflection between the hectic days of dealing with crowds. Still again, Jesus managed the sequence of events taking Him to the cross by revealing bit by bit the details of His future suffering.

A chair also has responsibility for the speed, spacing, and sequence of the governing process of a Christ-centered board. A full agenda makes pacing the speed of the items a major challenge to the leadership of the chair. Major items cannot be slighted, and minor items cannot dominate. Matters of consequence cannot be deferred, and inconsequential matters must be brushed by or transferred to the consent agenda.

Spacing is a companion of speed. In planning the agenda for board work, the white space of coffee and bathroom breaks goes along with decisions referring items back to the chief executive or board committees for more information. No board can function at full efficiency with a nonstop schedule through long days and late nights. Depletion of energy is a fact of life for groups as well as individuals. A perceptive chair will always be on alert to make sure that the board is functioning at its highest level of energy.

Then there is the challenge of management of sequence in the board process. Think of the board as a drama that begins with entangling issues that have to be encountered, complications that must be sorted out, a denouement or climax that has to be reached, and a resolution that must be worked through before coming to the close. Sitting in a chair labeled "Director," the chair knows that the board must go through each stage before the drama is complete. There can be no shortcuts. As Jesus said that the Son of Man must go through suffering on the way to the cross, so the board must work through the emotions and complications of issues before coming to a conclusion. If an entangling issue is rushed to climax without considering the complications, there will be no resolution and the conflict will resurface at a later time.

As we read the story of Jesus's life and ministry, we are awed by his attention to the dynamics of individual and group behavior. During an encounter with an individual, we read, "He knew what was in each person" (John 2:25). While trying to teach His disciples, we remember He asked, "What were you arguing about on the road?" (Mark 9:33) When being pressed by crowds, He felt for them as "sheep without a shepherd" (Matt. 9:36). To be an effective leader of a Christ-centered organization, the chair will want to ask God for similar gifts of discernment for understanding the roles of individual members along with the dynamics of the full board itself.

## Reading the Roles

Board members all play different roles depending upon their personalities as well as their positions, their emotions as well as their understanding, and their intuitions as well as their information. These roles will also change from time to time depending upon the issue being discussed and interactions among the board members. The scene is always in flux, sometimes bordering on chaos, so that the chair knows why someone likened board leadership to herding cats or pushing a chain. It helps measurably if the chair understands and respects role differentiation among board members.

Research into the roles of individuals in groups has resulted in sophisticated listings. Because of my fascination with social research, I resonate with Belbin's separation of functional roles of group members into the categories of Plant, Resource Investigator, Coordinator, Shaper, Monitor Evaluator, Team Worker, Implementer, Completer Finisher, and Specialist.[6] The list is too complicated for practical use. So, out of my experience as a chair, I prefer to simplify the categories of board members into Doers, Feelers, Blockers, and Sitters.

- **Doers** are members who are task-oriented. They initiate questions, seek information, ask for clarification, diagnose the issues, summarize the position, and ask for action: all with the purpose of getting the job done and the decision made.

- **Feelers** are members who are especially sensitive to personal emotions and interpersonal relations. They have antennae picking up signals of tension and respond with words of encouragement, conciliation, and harmony.

- **Blockers** can be the bane of the board and a major challenge to the leadership of the chair. They have a full quiver of negative arrows—taking a negative stand on any issue, invoking procedural roadblocks, dominating the discussion, criticizing as a matter of course, and withdrawing if they do not get their way.

- **Sitters** are not much better. Large boards have more than their share of those who warm a seat, buckle under pressure, cast a passive vote, and contribute little to the energy or the effectiveness of the organization.

Even in the Christ-centered ministry to which board members bring their personal commitment to Jesus Christ, the board chair has to deal with the reality and the predictability of these roles. It is easy to applaud the Doers, smooch the Feelers, condemn the Blockers, and ignore the Sitters. Stereotyping of persons or redlining of messages is beneath the expectations for Christ-centered leadership. Instead, the chair needs to understand their motivation, accept their differences, and foresee their potential for being part of a lively, interactive board that can come to an informed and convicted decision in support of the mission.

The chair must take on the unwritten assignment of knowing these board members personally, hearing their ambitions as well as their grievances, and drawing them into the larger purpose for which the ministry exists. Only in the case of a

Blocker becoming a saboteur who undercuts leadership or foments a dysfunctional board should the chair put his or her authority on the line for discipline or dismissal.

Like Jesus with the highly individualized company of Peter the Doer, John the Feeler, Thomas the Blocker, and Thaddeus the Sitter, the question is whether or not these diverse and contesting members can become a cohesive group moving as one toward the fulfillment of Jesus's redemptive mission. The answer is the same for Christ-centered board members as it was for Jesus's disciples. Despite their widespread differences, they must have the common characteristic of what A. W. Tozer calls "spiritual receptivity."[7] By being open to change in the will and way of God, individual differences can be transformed into a cohesive group achieving its intended goal.

## Transforming the Group

Research again leads the way into the dynamics of transforming individual differences into a powerful working group. Persons with experience as chairs of Christ-centered ministries will readily recognize the classic steps for group development authored by Thomas Buckman—Forming, Storming, Norming and Performing.[8] Every group goes through this process time and time again, depending upon its composition, changes in membership, shifts in the culture, and the issue at hand. Again, the chair must be a student of the process in order to lead in the development of a cohesive and effective board. In my book, I trace Buckman's four steps in detail and identify the role of the leader in each case.

**Forming** is the initial step when a new or changed board comes together to organize its members into various leadership roles and governing groups. As already noted, the chair takes the lead in the Forming stage; staffing the structure, appointing chairs, and making the charge for the working groups. Architects have a saying: "We build our buildings and then they build us." Board chairs need to take the cue and remember, "We form our boards and then they form us."

**Storming** is a stage in the transformation of groups from which Christ-centered organizations are not exempt. In fact, it is an error for a chair to assume that once a board is formed, cohesion will be automatic and unity will be assured. As board members test the water for their roles and interact with colleagues, interpersonal tensions will rise, pecking orders will be established, and conflicts will be inevitable.

Jesus went through the Storming stage with His own disciples when James and John asked if they could sit on His right and left hand when He formed the structure for His Kingdom. Other disciples heard what was going on and went into frenzy as ambition and jealousy collided. The same thing happens in Christ-centered ministries. As board members test out their position and power, they are bound to create short circuits in relationships. Officers of the board will exercise their authority in order to establish their position, chairs of committees to want to make their agenda high priority in full board sessions, and individual members will try to find their voice in the debate. Inevitably, strong feelings will be expressed with gains and losses.

The board chair who understands the Storming stage will not be dismayed. With deft strokes of diplomacy, the chair's role is to lift the sights of the contending board members to focus on the guiding mission and reinforce their self-esteem by emphasizing the part that each has to play in the fulfillment of their redemptive mission.

**Norming** is the process that calms the storm when boards are under development. More than that, it is the task that ultimately determines the quality of board leadership. No one can take the place of the chair in articulating the norms for board relationships and modeling those norms in the style and substance of leadership. Returning to Jesus's encounter with the disputing disciples over status in the Kingdom of God, He gives them the principle, "Whoever wants to become great among you must be your servant" (Mark 10:43) and then backs it up with Himself as the example: "For even the Son of Man did not come to be served, but to serve, and to give His life as a ransom for many" (Mark 10:45).

As board chair, Jesus is our model. The way out of the Storming stage of board development is the chair's statement of the servanthood principle with the evidence of his or her life and leadership.

**Performing** is described as the final stage when a cohesive board is working according to policy and arriving at informed decisions. A Christ-centered board is all of this and more. Cohesion is the key to its performance. A cohesive Christ-centered board is known for its:

- common identity in Christ;

- sole commitment to the Word of God;

- unqualified dependence upon the Holy Spirit;

- bond of relationship in the Body of Christ;

- shared sense of purpose in the Great Commission;

- servant spirit in supporting each other;

- satisfaction in working together; and

- celebration of wins, large and small, for the glory of God.

From the strength of cohesion comes the power for closure. The chair of the Christ-centered ministry must be a Finisher leading a fully-engaged board in timely fashion through to informed policy decisions that achieve its strategic goals and advance its God-given mission. On the way to that ideal, the chair will encounter crisis, conflict, and controversy; the stuff out of which character is made, for both the board and its members.

# 8

# MEDIATOR

*Guiding the board through the threats*
*of internal and external conflict*
*into the opportunities for resolution, management,*
*and transformation as witness*
*of reconciliation in the Body of Christ.*

Conflict is proof that the Christ-centered ministry is alive and well. Whether its source is internal or external, it must be addressed. It cannot be avoided, and it carries the danger of becoming toxic. Think of conflict for the board as we think about failure for the chief executive. It is an opportunity for learning rather an occasion for despair. The board chair presides over the choice. Resolution of the conflict matures a board; failure exposes a dysfunctional board.

## Source of Conflict

The challenge of conflict for a board can come from either internal or external sources, related to purpose, policy, procedure, or people. My experience as chair of a Christ-centered ministry is more specific.

Internal conflict for the Christ-centered ministry tends to come from matters related to management, theology, or finance. Management issues most often involve problems of character or competence. Theological matters were usually divided between conservative or liberal positions on details of policy or practice. Financial matters drew conflict over the allocation of limited resources. Frequently, these conflicts became personal as board members took sides or strong members championed different positions.

External conflict tends to be intergroup rather than inter-personal. Again, experience speaks. Challenges that come to the Christ-centered board from external sources are led by matters of religious freedom, conformity to governmental regulations, qualifications for professional associations, concerns from the constituency, and pressure from the prevailing culture.

I vividly recall board contests over the requirement for including creed along with age, race, and gender in the required statement of the EEOC nondiscrimination and the related question of whether or not the Christ-centered ministry can limit its hiring to committed Christians. Other challenges came from self-regulation of professional accrediting and credentialing agencies, both secular and religious, whose recognition adds credibility to the ministry and its staff members.

## Leading Through Conflict

While the leadership role of the chair must be nuanced for every conflict, internal or external, there are steps that apply to every crisis or conflict.

**Step 1. Confront.** Our high hopes for the Christ-centered ministry can lead to the false assumption that conflict does not exist or must be avoided at all cost. A chair who takes that position does a disservice to the board. Any person who has served as a director or trustee of a Christ-centered ministry will recall meetings when the elephant in the room lurked over, above, and behind the agenda. Deaf ears, bland voices, and uninspired decisions characterized the meeting.

It is false hope to assume that the crisis will go away by avoidance. Early on, I learned that it is the responsibility of the chair to confront the hidden issue. Otherwise, it grows and festers until it is a conflict threatening the very existence of the board.

**Step 2. Clarify.** Bringing a controversial issue into the open is risky business. To avert the natural tendency toward emotional responses, the chair must objectify the issue with a clarifying statement. With the Spirit-guided gift of discernment, the chair must identify the substantive core of the issue, note the emotional strings that are attached, and frame the key questions in a manageable context for discussion and decision. Board members especially appreciate leaders who bring clarity to controversial issues. Increased respect and added trust will be the result.

**Step 3. Confirm.** After confronting and clarifying the issue, it is an opportune time for the chair to remind the board members of the mission and vision to which they are called and which they must protect as well as advance. Otherwise, the crisis or conflict can become an all-consuming issue that diverts the board from its primary purpose. The chair's confirmation will also serve as a lodestar in dealing with the crisis or conflict.

During the frank and sometimes heated discussion that may follow, the chair can intervene at critical times with a reminder of the mission and vision to which the board is pledged.

**Step 4. Communicate.** Once the chair has brought the pending crisis or conflict out into the open and placed the issue within the context of mission and vision of the board, it is time to talk it out. Boards that have developed a climate of lively discussion engaging all of the members will have a head start toward the resolution of conflict. Otherwise, the chair may have to preside over a cacophony of strident voices defying consensus or compromise.

The opposite can also happen. Some board members will want to stonewall the issue or sweep it under the rug. At this point, the chair's leadership style comes into play. Directive Chairs will tromp on the process, and Collaborative Chairs will rely on participation for resolution. When all is said and done, a crisis or conflict will tend to reinforce the leadership style of the chair. A time of crisis or conflict is a call for the chair to lead the board into a learning experience for all and become a change agent for improving the communication process.

**Step 5. Contemplate.** Every intense discussion comes to a moment when members of a Christ-centered board need to exercise the spiritual discipline of stepping away from the issue and seeking the mind of God. At the call of the chair, a time of silence, a period of prayer, or a recess for solitude give board members the perspective they need.

William Ury calls this time of contemplation "going to balcony." We can imagine ourselves sitting in the balcony, looking down on the debate, and gaining a perspective of the larger picture in which the pieces fit together. Ury's books *Getting to Yes* and *Getting Past No* are on my list of required reading for board chairs.[9] Wrap his wise words in the Spirit-guided sensitivity for the board chair of a Christ-centered ministry and going to the balcony becomes one of the most effective tools for leadership. Without exception, I can say that every time I called for a break in controversial discussions so that we could gain the perspective of the balcony, the board came back together and worked its way to resolution.

**Step 6. Conciliate.** At this point in the process, the chair must bring the Spirit-guided gift of discernment to the resolution of conflict. Leadership begins with sorting the issues into three categories of conflict. First, there are *intra-group* conflicts that can be resolved in support of the mission and vision of the Christ-centered ministry. A case in point is the policy decision on whether or not to require that all employees, including staff and service people, be committed Christians. The right of religious freedom is at stake.

Second, there are *inter-group* conflicts that can only be contained, not resolved. An example is the decision of whether or not to accept financial aid from governmental sources in order to advance the ministry. Christ-centered ministries in education, international relief, medical services, and domestic welfare all face this question.

Third, there are *interpersonal* conflicts that needed to transformed by the spiritual experiences of forgiveness and reconciliation. Heated board debates that lead too harsh words and personal attacks fit this category. In each of these cases, the board Chair holds responsibility to sort out the issues and propose the path from conflict to conciliation.

**Step 7. Closure.** Conflict is contagious. Unless there is closure for the issue, it will continue to spread its toxic influence through the board and beyond, even to the staff and constituents of the Christ-centered ministry. Once again, the chair has to take the lead in bringing the controversy to a close. Depending upon the nature of the issue, three options for closure come into view:

- *Conflict resolution* is the option for substantive issues that relate to policy and procedures. After the board has thoroughly discussed the issues and weighed the options for resolution, the chair calls for closure by consensus or majority decision. Once the board votes its mind, the issue is resolved, and the chair calls all members to speak with one voice. A decision on the allocation of limited resources is an example. After the push and pull of conflicting needs, the decision that is made is final.

- *Conflict management* maybe necessary for intractable issues, particularly when those issues arise from external sources over which the board has no control. The constant threat to religious liberty is a case in point. The board cannot bring final resolution by consensus or majority vote, but it can remain on alert and manage its application to the policies and programs of the ministry.

- *Conflict transformation* is the hope that the Christ-centered ministry holds for interpersonal issues. No one disputes the fact that Christians are persons of strong convictions—and sometimes perpetrators of prejudice in the erroneous interpretation of truth. The difference, however, is the intervention of the Holy Spirit calling for confession and forgiveness. Whether through the informal means of getting adversaries together for a personal meeting or proposing the formal process of biblical reconciliation, the board chair leads in overseeing the transformational process.

Here we stand. The call of the chair to be a Mediator is an honor conferred on a leader who has earned the trust required to confront conflict and bring it through a teaching-learning process to closure that builds the board of the Christ-centered ministry. Pitfalls are always present, and risk is par for the course. Conflict is a challenge that tests spiritual maturity at its very core. To be up to the challenge, a board chair must be in tune with the mind of Christ, sensitive to the promptings of His Spirit, and ready to do the will of God without regard for personal cost.

## 9

# MONITOR

*Assessing the performance of the board*
*according to the principles of good governance,*
*achievement of the God-given mission,*
*and the personal/professional/spiritual growth of its members.*

Assessment is the task that ultimately defines the effectiveness of the Christ-centered board. Why, then, do boards tend to shy away from this task? Why are the tools for assessment so seldom used? Why doesn't the task include assessment of the board itself?

Answers to these questions come to rest in the role of the board chair. Unless the chair manages the assessment of the board, its members, its chief executive, and the chair itself, it will not be done. An awakening call is needed in Christ-centered ministries for making assessment one of the standards of good practice that will directly affect not just the effectiveness of the board but its credibility in a culture that is increasingly skeptical of faith-based ministries.

# Assessing Our Assessment

Thinking back to the boards on which I have served or as led as chair, I confess that assessment is one of the dullest tools in our leadership kit. Things are changing as advances in leadership theory and practice are adopted by Christ-centered ministries and their boards.

Assessment of chief executive officers is now an expected procedure, even though it is still uneven and often spasmodic. Board assessment lags farther behind. Many boards give the responsibility to a committee on governance or to the executive committee. Formal assessment with consultation is usually reserved for crisis situations.

I recall a crisis that cut short my sabbatical. It was an in-house issue until one of the protagonists decided to use the local media as a weapon against the opposition. It is no exaggeration to say that all hell broke loose, and a distress call came to our quiet retreat in the desert. We resolved the issue but not without pain and loss. As we debriefed on the background and circumstances that brought the matter to the crisis stage, we realized that the magnitude of the issue required the formal engagement of a consultant to make an objective assessment and propose recommendations so that it would not happen again.

Years later I witnessed another campus implode in crisis. Internal assessment failed, and outside consultation was brought in. Now, in reflection on both cases, I realize that a chair who encouraged regular and occasionally formal assessment of internal relationships among board members and with the chief executive might have prevented the crises that followed.

With a chuckle, I also remember my attempt as chief executive to take the lead in a plan to make assessment a standard throughout the organization, beginning with the board and sweeping through the ranks of administration and faculty all the way to support staff. The announcement of my request for evaluation won widespread applause, but no one stepped up to join me. In fact, the plan backfired when I proposed a five-year rolling review for faculty members. Tenured faculty in particular interpreted the meaning of tenure to be assessment free, except by peer review of their scholarly publications.

Assessment as a developmental tool is perceived as a threat, particularly among professional specializations. It cannot be forced from the top down, and it will not be chosen from the bottom up. Only as all participants in Christ-centered ministries come together in collaborative agreement will assessment be perceived as an opportunity rather than a threat.

Here is where the board chair comes into play again. Assessment cannot stand alone as an organizational requirement. It must be part of the total package of personal, professional, and spiritual development for every person and written into the policy manual related to human resources. Even more important, assessment must lead to a growth plan for every person and be backed up by the resources of time and money to make it feasible. Although it will take time to put the full package together and longer yet to get everyone on board, the chair has the opportunity to sound the affirmative call as a spiritual commitment of the board to all whose lives are invested in the Christ-centered mission.

# Assessment of Excellence

*Are we exceeding the standards of good practice in all of our policies and practices?*

Good practices are not good enough for the Christ-centered ministry. If we are "letters to be read of all men," as the Apostle Paul reminds us, excellence should be the standard of our witness. We fall short of that standard if our policies and practices in finance barely get a clean audit, staff are treated as "personnel," fundraising pushes the margins of administrative costs, and marketing stays just within the boundaries of overstatement.

Because the secular world relishes the news of scandal in the Christian community, Christ-centered ministries carry the same weighty responsibility as individual Christians for being a squeaky clean witness to the world. When scandal breaks out in the political world, pundits say, "None of us can afford to be frisked." Ask the question of ourselves and the Christ-centered ministry: "Can any of us afford to be frisked?" No one claims perfection for Christians or Christ-centered ministries, but all can claim the expectation that we are striving for excellence in every area of our lives.

The board chair is custodian of that expectation. Whether overseeing the assessment of the board, its members, or its chief executive, the chair is the one who presses for excellence of Christian witness beyond the standards of good practice.

# Assessment of Coherence

*Are we seeing our God-given purpose revealed in every aspect of our ministry?*

We make no apology for coming back to this question repeatedly. Without a continuing focus on the primary purpose of a Christ-centered ministry, the very nature of organizational behavior tends toward pockets of self-interest, silos of power, and fiefdoms of competing leaders. It is up to the chair to keep the image of the unified Body of Christ before the board and give support to the chief executive in decisions that heal the fractures. No ministry is whole until all of the parts are playing from the same page.

Even as I write, media reports the demotion and resignation of a university president because he failed to handle the allegations of sexual assaults in the athletic department. My heart reaches out to him because I have walked in his shoes. Untouchable fiefdoms of athletics are a fact of life in Christ-centered colleges and universities that a president takes on at the risk of his position.

Similar issues can plague every Christ-centered ministry. Because constituencies have favorites, board members have egos, and individual administrators have agendas; it is up to the board chair to assess these situations and call for coherence as a witness of the faith. If the call for coherence goes unheeded, the board chair will have no choice but to recommend incision of the rebellious member. A personal price will be paid, but that is the risk that goes with the job.

## Assessment of Wholeness

*Are we developing personal, professional, and spiritual wholeness in the people who are investing their lives in our ministry?*

Again, the board chair needs to make no apology for repeatedly reinforcing the commitment of the Christ-centered ministry to development of whole persons. Assessment will follow the call. The morale of board members, the chief executive, and staff is a ready indicator of whether or not persons find meaning in their roles and satisfaction in their results.

We cannot forget that members of the board are volunteers giving their time, energy, and money because they believe in the Christ-centered ministry. Their reward is the satisfaction of doing God's will and growing in His grace. Even though the assessment of board members' satisfaction and growth is rare, it is easily measured by their attendance, engagement, and staying power for board meetings. A chair with sensitive antennae will quickly pick up signals of morale on a rising or falling tide.

There is also merit in engaging the services of the Best Christian Workplaces Institute, with its proven instrument of staff assessment to measure the health of the organization individually and corporately. Al Lopus, President of BCPWI, notes that the health of an organization may be "its most important asset" and just as important to measure as its financial audit.

Board chairs of Christ-centered ministries have a special obligation to put the development of whole persons at the top of their assessment agenda. Wholeness and holiness are companions in the faith. Throughout scripture, this truth is at the center of revelation, beginning with wholeness of God's first creation in Genesis and the holiness of God's final creation in Revelation. In between, wholeness as holiness is the dominant theme of the patriarchs and prophets of the Old Testament and of Jesus, Paul, and the Apostles in the New Testament. Everything comes to focus in the development of a "servant of God...thoroughly equipped for every good work"

(II Tim. 3:17). To strive for that goal is to justify the existence of the Christ-centered organization.

## Assessment of Acclaim

*Are we giving God the glory for our honors and achievements?*

A major difference between Christ-centered ministries and for-profit or nonprofit organizations is in the question, "Who gets the credit?" Profit-making entities honor chief executive officers who exceed expectations on the bottom line. Nonprofit institutions give recognition to volunteer citizens with a heart for meeting a social need. Christ-centered ministries may honor both professional executives and citizen volunteers, but always within the context of giving the greater glory to God.

In the routine of business and with the drag of perfunctory decisions, a board can forget the ultimate purpose of its existence. The chair, however, must never forget this purpose. The chair's portfolio of assessments includes the question to be asked of small wins and large gains: "Who gets the credit?" No matter what the rest of the world thinks, "To God be the glory" is the motto on the masthead of the flag that flies over the Christ-centered ministry.

# MASTER

*Being alert for warning signs of action by Board members or the Board itself that deviate from the purpose or undercut the integrity of the Christ-centered ministry.*

No one comes to the position as chair of the board of a Christ-centered ministry with a mastery of the role. Gifts that are cultivated and skills that are learned in other leadership positions help, but direct transfer is limited. Experience is the teacher.

Boards of Christ-centered ministries are like the families described by Leo Tolstoy: "All happy families are alike; each unhappy family is unhappy in its own way."[10] We have already identified the qualities that make happy boards—trust, integrity, coherence, and accountability. Board leadership requires a level of mastery for each of these virtues. Equally important, the board chair must become an expert in reading the warning signs that create an unhappy family, either by the actions of individual board members or the board itself.

Trust, integrity, coherence, and accountability are fragile virtues, hard to gain and easy to lose. When these virtues are at stake, the mastery of the board chair is put to test. Will the chair be the board-authorized point of control to manage the issue and assure the integrity of the organization? Out of personal experience, I offer these cautions that require masterful leadership by the chair of the board of the Christ-centered ministry.

## The Dysfunctional Board Member

Individual board members are bound by written and unwritten codes of conduct. Relationships among board members of Christ-centered ministries put these codes to test because of the family, business, and church connections through which communication flows. Violations are seldom intentional, but they can be destructive to the integrity of the board. The board chair must be especially alert to three red flags that fly and be ready to deal with them.

**Board Bypass.** The relational strengths of the Christ-centered board have a downside. When everyone knows everyone else and sees each other frequently outside of board meetings, confidential or privileged information can be leaked either intentionally or unintentionally.

Intentional leaks come from ego-driven motives. Under the guise of personal confidence, the board members let a family member, friend or colleague in on the latest scoop related to board direction or a decision. In one organization, the board members were so tightly bound in their Christian relationship that we had to operate from the premise that everyone knew everything. In such circumstances, the board chair is the one to make confidentiality a moral commitment for each board member as part of the oath of office. If that commitment is violated, the board chair has to call out the violation in personal conference and reinforce the moral code in general sessions.

**Conflict of Interest.** Multiple precautions are taken to avoid conflicts of interests by individual board members. Bylaws and policy manuals will carry detailed descriptions of potential conflicts, and annual documents require signed agreements to prevent the problem.

Usually, we think of conflicts of interest in the realm of finance and business. As a board chair, I had to ask a longtime and beloved patriarch to decide between board membership and compensation as an adjunct advancement officer. In another case, it became my duty to quiet the storm when the board required open bidding for a service contract that had been held exclusively by one of its members for years.

Conflicts of interest go beyond financial issues. A firestorm brewed when a board member talked "in confidence" with a colleague about a change in financial strategy. Another time, a board member appealed for an exception in the board's discipline of a rebellious son.

Each of these conflicts had the sensitivity of a festering boil and, as chair, I had to learn a lesson. Overreaction would cause irreparable hurt, and inattention would open the door to further abuse. Mastery cannot be claimed, because every conflict of interest is different, but if ever the board chair needs the discerning mind of Spirit, these are the times.

**Violation of Authority.** No board policy is more basic than the non-negotiable dictum that board members, including the chair, have no authority in themselves. Only as the action of the full board is affirmed can an individual member say, "By authority of the board." Even in Christ-centered ministries, the board chair will have occasion to remind its members that no one has an individual voice. The policy may seem obvious, but it can be violated.

A board member who disliked an internal decision told the staff administrator, "Remember who signs your paycheck." This clear violation of individual authority wreaked havoc with confidence in the board, and the chair had act on behalf of the executive committee to confront the member. Another board member asked for special privileges in engaging the services of the organization. Hidden behind the request was the assumed authority of an individual member. Responsibility again fell to the board chair to meet with the person and reaffirm the principle. No easy job, but the board chair is at the point of control and must be master of the situation.

## The Dysfunctional Board

Unhappy boards do not stumble into dysfunction. Like the Distant Early Warning Line that protected the United States and Canada from attack during the Cold War, there are distant early warnings of which the board chair must be aware. Patrick Lencioni, in his book *The Five Dysfunctions of a Team*, sees those warnings as the links of a chain leading to dysfunction: (1) absence of trust, (2) fear of conflict, (3) lack of commitment, (4) avoidance of accountability, and (5) inattention to results.[11] So, while it is true that an unhappy board is unhappy in its own way, there warnings. The following examples of a dysfunctional board attest to fact that the warnings must be heeded.

**Kicking the Can.** For some reason, Christ-centered boards are prone to "kick the can" down the road and let a future generation deal with a difficult issue. Often, financial viability is the can to be kicked. A classic case comes to mind from Christian higher education. A university president convinced the board to freeze tuition and increase institutionally funded student aid under the premise, "You lose a bit on each student but make it up in volume." It didn't take long for the can to kick back.

Nor can we forget the notorious New Era Foundation scam that sucked in gullible leaders of Christ-centered boards who saw a ready return from the pyramid scheme. I served on the board of a Christ-centered ministry when the chief executive, with the support of the board chair, recommended investing gifts from the constituency in the scheme, with its promise of multiple returns. It became my lot to oppose the recommendation as a gamble with God's money which had been given, often at sacrifice, by the constituents of the ministry. The proposal lost, and the ministry escaped the chaos that followed.

The fact is that the field of ministry is full of consultants with programs promising rich returns. Boards, particularly in a time when competition for limited resources is so tense, are vulnerable to a "kick the can" decision. Chief executives, under the gun for financial solvency, are also susceptible. The board chair is often the court of last resort with the perspective for longterm accountability. It is a point of control that comes with mastery of the situation.

**March of Folly.** Recently, I reread Barbara Tuchman's book, *The March of Folly*, in which she retraces such world-changing disasters as Rheaboam's loss of the Ten Tribes, the Trojans' use of a wooden horse, and the United States' defeat in Vietnam.[12] In each case, a leadership decision made by a person or a group illustrates "policy pursued contrary to self-interest."[13] Even when the policy produces catastrophic results, the group ego persists in "woodenheadedness" that aggravates the crisis and causes seismic shifts in the culture.[14]

The March of Folly is not limited to ancient history or international affairs. Boards of Christ-centered ministries have been known to pursue policy contrary to self-interest and persist in woodenheadedness that has a longterm, negative effect upon the ministry. Oftentimes these decisions are theological. We have seen denominational factions stomp on institutions that do not subscribe to their radical position. We have seen boards of Christ-centered ministries trade the distinction of mission for the sake of government approval, legal resolution, or financial aid. We have also seen boards grow lax in discipline by the entitlement of endowments. These examples are another part of the distant early warning system for the boards and chairs of Christ-centered ministries.

No prophetic wisdom is needed to predict that issues testing both the consequences of policy and the willingness to confess error are bursting all over the contemporary scene. While the responsibility for decisions in these matters will begin with the chief executive and end in the hands of the board, the chair is the one who needs to call for consideration of the consequences. We have already noted that the board chair must ask every time the board makes a decision, "Is this consistent with our mission?" Now, we add the companion question, "What are the long-term consequences of this policy?" The chair who keeps asking these questions will be a leader worthy of the call.

**Fingers in the Tent.** A thin line separates a policy-making board from one accused of micromanaging. As a guide to the difference, we invoke the analogy "nose in, fingers out." The board of a Christ-centered ministry has to have a nose to sniff out what is happening internally within the areas of executive authority, but it cannot follow the smell of the nose with the touch of the fingers.

The temptation is ever-present. Whenever the board takes it upon itself to bypass the chief executive and involve itself in executive matters, the fingers are in the tent. In one disappointing moment, I heard a chief executive describe the prolonged and painful process of working with a staff member in divorce proceedings. The case came to the board as a matter of confidential information, but some board members felt as if divorce was always an open and shut case. Rather than expressing confidence in the chief executive dealing with the ongoing crisis, the board overruled the chief executive and enacted a policy against divorce by staff members, ruling it as retroactive in the case. Ultimately, micromanaging by the board cost the chief executive his job.

In another instance, the board of a Christ-centered ministry heard a report from a standing committee recommending an across-the-board salary increase above the chief executives' recommendation. Committee members failed to recognize that a tight budget had been worked and reworked to bring it into balance according to the policy of board. Without revenues to cover the salary increase, the committee put the chief executive into an untenable position. Only after an impassioned appeal by the chief executive did the board shelve the committee's recommendation.

One chief executive tells the humorous story about the board chair announcing, "I am retiring so that I can spend more time on the campus." You can understand why the chief executive said, "I knew that I was in trouble." His prediction proved true. The board chair interpreted his role in retirement as contacting administrative and staff members to ask, "How are things going?"

Believe it or not, there is a time when the board has to put its fingers in the tent, and I have been the culprit. In one of my presidencies, I had a conflict with the board over a policy decision for new program development that outran the resources and the readiness of the institution to make the leap. Despite my appeal for a change in timing, the board chose to go forward. When I reported the outcome to a faculty that was in strong opposition to the move, I softened the mandate and inferred that we still had time for planning. Word of my report went straight up the pipeline to the board. An altar call followed, with the board chair acting on behalf of the executive committee. I was given a choice: either follow the mandate of the board or resign my position. Because I believed that the board was right to expect its chief executive to follow its command unless a legal or ethical matter was involved, I apologized for my failure to accurately report the board action. The board's clarification of the situation with the faculty added hostility to their opposition, and their disgruntlement continued until success of the venture finally brought reconciliation. Only in rare instances such as this should the board put its fingers into the tent.

Mastery as a point of control is fraught with danger. Jesus encountered scribes who used their mastery of the Law as a tool for justifying sin and exploiting people. At its extreme, control is a weapon of leadership that turns on itself and becomes evil rather than good. Jesus countered with sharp words that exposed their hypocrisy and shamed them with the call to self-sacrifice. His lesson is still with us. Only for the board chair who has the discerning mind and humble spirit of Jesus Christ will mastery be obedient to the Master.

# PART III

---

# ARTISTRY
# OF THE CHAIR

# 11

# MAESTRO

*Orchestrating the functions, relationships,
and decisions of board governance into a
harmonious whole that glorifies God.*

Missionary, Model, Mentor, Manager, Moderator, Mediator,
Monitor, and Master—the many faces and functions of the
board chair are before us like pieces of a puzzle on a table.
How do we put them together?

Late in my career I had an "Aha" experience while reading
Roger Nierenberg's little book *Maestro*.[15] It is the story of an
executive who learns how to lead from the conductor of an
orchestra. The message is clear: leadership is more than science.
It is art, and the goal of leadership is more than a list of
achievements; it is the sound of music. For the first time, I saw
the board chair's leadership in its spiritual potential. With full
credit to the author, I applied the message of *Maestro* to the role
of the board chair of a Christ-centered ministry and then put
it into practice. Like the conductor of a symphony orchestra,
I prepared myself for board meetings by asking the questions
that see leadership as an art and the sound of music as its goal.

**Do I lead with vision?** A conductor comes to a rehearsal or performance with more than a detailed understanding of the musical score. In the conductor's imagination is the sound of the music when all of the instruments are playing as one, and this artistic meaning transcends technique. As a board chair, I always brought full preparation to the meetings where I presided, but I did not imagine the outcome of the board working in concert as a community. The agenda served as a worksheet for numerous items to be addressed. We chipped them off one at a time, each item standing on its own with little connection to the previous or next item. Our goal was to complete the agenda, not to work toward a vision.

A variation on an old story illustrates the transforming power of a vision. A custodian mopping at NASA in the 1960s was asked, "What are you doing?" He answered, "I am putting a man on the moon."[16]

The truth still stands. As board chair, I can lead by completing an agenda or by creating a vision. If I come to the board meeting foreseeing the body working in concert as a community, the vision will give direction to my leadership. By intention and inference, every agenda item will lead toward that vision and become part of the whole.

**Do I gain perspective from my position?** A raised podium is perceived by most of us in the audience as a position of power from which the conductor controls the orchestra. Not so, according to the teacher in *Maestro*, who says that the primary purpose of the elevated position is to give the conductor the perspective of the whole.[17] Board chairs do not need a podium to gain perspective. From a central position at the table, they have the advantage of seeing every face.

At one board meeting, I was seated at the center of a long table with three board members on each side. Only as I stretched to the left or right could I see their faces and acknowledge their presence. So I took a time-out and changed the shape of the table so that I could see the faces of all board members, and they could see mine. Unwittingly, perhaps, I had an intuitive grasp of the conductor's place on the podium. By seeing the faces of all board members, I could acknowledge their presence, hear their voices, read their faces, and relate their responses to the vision of community.

My greatest frustration came when I took the chair for a thirty-five-member board. In our first meeting, the members were seated in double rows, one behind another. The situation was impossible, so once again I exercised the chair's prerogative to reorganize the room. A giant circle was created, permitting me to see every member and every member to see each other. It helped, but it still put a drag on the vision of the board working in concert as a community. Personalities took over, and factions developed. My vision as chair took a hit, and it was all that I could do to hold the group together. In such situations, the board chair deserves a podium.

**Is everyone reading from the same page?** As simple as it seems, the greatest strength of an orchestral conductor is the fact that everyone is playing from the same page.[18] The question is to how interpret the score, not rewrite it. With boards of Christ-centered ministry, this can be a problem. Even if a board member has read the materials sent out in advance, there is the temptation to rewrite it, add to it, or propose a substitute. As noted earlier, these intentions should be expressed when the board chair asks the members for additions to the proposed agenda. Legitimate items should be merged into the schedule and others referred for advanced consideration. At this point, the chair can then call for assent on the agenda as proposed and go forward by asking, "Are we all on the same page?" Informal agreement should set the board free to focus its attention on the agenda as revised and confirmed. In other words, the board must own the agenda before the meeting proceeds.

What is the page to which board members will give full attention? Without hesitation we go back to the collaborative agreement between the board chair and the chief executive on the recommendations that will advance the mission, vision, and strategic plan of the ministry. If any board member has another agenda, it must be advanced when the chair asks for other items of business.

Still, debate can wander and subconscious motives can surface. Another arrow in the quiver of the board chair is to repeat the question, "Are we still on the same page?" If a board wanders from the mutual recommendations of its chair and chief executive, the vision for community becomes a doubtful hope.

**Is everyone tuned to the same note?** Playing on the same page must be matched by being tuned to the same note. In the orchestral field, it is the concertmaster who strikes the note of A to which all the instruments are tuned.[19] The slightest variation of the purity of that tone creates discord in the orchestra. To assure the purity of tone, the conductor defers to the concertmaster to strike the note that calls all members of the orchestra into agreement.

Without pressing the analogy too far, I see the board chair as conductor of the score who defers to the chief executive as concertmaster to set the tone. As soon as the agenda is set, the chair turns the meeting over to the chief executive for a report with recommendations for action. The text of the chief executive's report gives the chair the score to be conducted, and the tone gives the chair the keynote of tone that will guide the meeting.

As a former chief executive, I confess to succumbing to the temptation to set a tone that is overly optimistic. The assumption is that the board only wants to hear good news. However, as Max DePree reminds us, the first responsibility of a leader is to "define reality."[20]

Once again, we are up against the fact that current reality sounded against a strategic vision can be a unifying note of hope. Like a symphony that goes through movements of storm and stress as well as peace and clam, the same note carries through. As part of their collaborative preparation for the board meeting, the chair and chief executive will agree on the common tone as well as the common text.

**Am I listening to the parts?** The conductor of an orchestra has the advantage of seeing the different players in their sections with their instruments. With a look of the eye and a turn of the head, the conductor can hear each of these parts, and with a wave of the baton or a look of the eye, modulate the sound. A board chair may not have the advantage of listening to defined sections with visible instruments among the members, but a perceptive ear will sort them out. Financiers, theologians, educators, attorneys, entrepreneurs, consultants, medical doctors, and corporate leaders are like sections in the orchestra of the Christ-centered organization whose voices must all be heard. As the first lesson of the conductor in *Maestro*, he told the corporate executive, "Listen to the clarinet," perhaps the most forgotten instrument in a symphony.[21]

A board chair must also hear the lesser voices among the members of the Christ-centered board. Some are reluctant to speak because of their personality or feelings of inferiority. Others get engulfed by the dominance of more articulate members. It is up to the board chair to make sure that all of the voices are heard. Like major players hearing the sound of the clarinet in an orchestra, when the lesser voices of a Christ-centered board are heard, there is greater potential for the sound of artistic harmony.

**Are the parts listening to each other?** The gentle admonition to listen to the clarinet applies to board members as well as the board chair. It is one thing for the chair to hear all of the voices of the board and quite another to make sure that the members are listening to each other.

With regret, I remember times in board meetings when the lesser were ignored or tolerated as necessary to be heard but irrelevant to the conversation. As board chair, I should have stopped the discussion and asked the question, "Are we hearing each other?" Or I could have affirmed the lesser voice by saying, "Let's hear more of what you have to say." If we are really working together toward a collaborative community, the board chair will hear every voice, and every voice will hear each other.

**Do I feel the flow into the future?** Board meetings are movements with varying speeds and varying steps. Every board has times when the movement stops and the body is stymied as well as moments when progress is frustrated because of stutter steps. Most memorable, however, are the instances of the board carrying on its business with a unifying flow into the future.

In *Maestro*, we learn that the conductor leads in three times zones—the score written the past, the music performed in the present, and the artistic meaning foreseen in the future.[22] It is the task of the conductor to create the flow among these time zones by leading the future. Here is where the baton comes into play. We might think of the wave of the baton as a point of control for the orchestra, but it is the tip of the baton that points to the future.

Boards can get stuck in the past, obsessed with the present, and forgetful about the future. If so, there is no flow. Even though the board chair does not wield a baton, there are other ways to keep the tip of leadership pointed to the future. Periodically, for instance, the chair can refer to the initial vision that was projected at the start of the meeting. Sometimes a restatement of the vision will be a correction from deviance in the subject or tone of meeting. At other times, it will serve as a stimulus to keep going forward into the future. Flow is the feeling of advancing in rhythmic steps into that future.

**Am I leading with a light touch?** When a symphony orchestra is playing with flow, it hardly needs a conductor. With just the lightest touch from the tip of the baton and a radiant smile on the face, the conductor enters into a zone of exhilaration. As a sailor, I liken it to the moment when all of the sails are in full sync with the wind and the captain needs only the lightest touch on the tiller to guide the boat. In *Maestro*, Nierenberger improves on that image by quoting Buckminster Fuller, architect of the geodesic dome, who likened the rare moment in artistic development when a battleship can steered with a trim tab on the rudder.[23]

The image carries over into a board meeting and the leadership of the chair. You can tell when a board is flowing in its movement by the chair's light touch of leadership. If a heavy hand is needed, you can be sure that the board is either out of control or off course. The guiding principle, according to *Maestro*, is "minimum necessary intervention."[24]

**Are we celebrating community?** Everything the conductor does is aimed at seeing the vision of a vivid imagination translated with depth of meaning and heights of joy through the sound of music. It happens only when the full orchestra works together as a collaborative community.

The author of *Maestro* uses a team-building exercise to illustrate a diverse group of individuals being transformed into a harmonious community.[25] In this exercise, each member has two rocks placed in front of him or her. On cue, the member picks up the rocks, clicks them together, puts them down, claps his or her hands, passes the rocks to person on the left, and picks up the next set of rocks. Individual and collective coordination is needed for the exercise. As would be expected, first attempts at the exercise produce a host of laughs and groans as some members bumble the individual steps and others fail at the passing game. Rocks pile up in front of some persons, and others do their part with lightning speed. After practice, the members improve their skills, communication improves, flow starts, and the sense of being a team takes hold. Finally, the time comes when all members are working together in the rhythm of clicking stones and coordinated passes. It is a moment to be remembered in the collaborative art of community.

In a symphony, the sound of music reaches the spheres, the message is conveyed, the emotions are stirred, and the vision of the conductor is realized. As chair of the board, why not anticipate that same sense of community in a business meeting when the spirit of the session rises above the agenda, unifies the members, gives rhythm to the proceedings, relates all decisions to the vision, and leaves the members with the satisfaction of being part of something significant?

**Has the vision become reality?** Maestro concludes with the conductor summing up leadership for business executives who attended his rehearsal:

> If you are a leader, if you stand on a podium, if you hold in your hand a baton, then it falls on your shoulders to make remarkable things happen. You mustn't settle for a series of satisfactory transactions. You can elevate your team to heights beyond their wildest imagination. [26]

Yes, when vision becomes reality in an orchestral performance or a board meeting, something remarkable happens that goes beyond expectations. Science rises to art, rationality gives way to mystery, and routine is surprised by wonder. The impact is profound when the vision resonates with the depth of human experience, the parts become whole, and fact partners with emotion. I liken this moment to rereading the text of something that I have written and out of wonder exclaim, "Did I write that?" As rare as those moments may be, they are unforgettable, indelible, and transforming.

What is the role of the board chair in these moments? Go back to Max Depree's crowning statement for leadership. He says that the first responsibility of a leader is to "define reality; the final responsibility is to say thank you, and in between to be debtor to all."[26] The grittiest task of a chair is to pay the debt to all by the self-sacrifice that reconciles fractures and redeems failures in the mystery and hope of a transcending vision. This is only way in which the team—whether a symphony orchestra, a business enterprise, or a faith-based ministry—is elevated to heights beyond imagination.

A special moment awaits an orchestra that has brought a transforming vision to reality. The conductor asks all of the members to stand for applause and then points out the sections one by one with a personal nod of appreciation. The chair has the same opportunity when the work of the board rises to spiritual dimensions. It is time to close the circle of leadership and say thank you. Provision should be made in the agenda for the chair to speak final words of assessment and appreciation. Thanks can be given to individuals, committees, and the general board who excelled in achievement of the vision. With these words, the door of the past is closed and the door of the future is opened.

## The Transcendent Moment

Is there any other crowning event that matches or exceeds the transforming experience of a great symphony? Is there a time in human history when we remember an empowering vision, a common score, a harmonious tune, a listening ear, a flow into the future, a collaborative community, a hope-filled message, a remarkable result, and a standing ovation as a turning point for the world?

116

Pentecost is the answer. Go back to the visionary evidence of that event when 120 disciples waited together as one—mysterious winds, flaming tongues, speaking voices, listening ears, prompting of the Spirit, and common understanding of God's mighty works. Pentecost is a transcendent experience filled with surprise, couched in mystery, and beyond human explanation. The vision then becomes reality in the character of the New Testament Church—being of one accord, hearing the Word, responding to teaching, having all things common, sacrificing for the needy, breaking bread together, fearing the Lord, witnessing signs and wonders, celebrating with gladness and simplicity, praising God, holding favor with all people, and adding daily to their numbers.

Astute readers will notice that each step in the Maestro's leadership breathes the spirit of something greater than the routine of a commendable performance or the work of a gifted leader. The audience awaits a transforming orchestral experience. For the Christ-centered ministry, the expectation is even greater. In its board meeting, the stage is set for the Holy Spirit, working through the chair, to lift the highest and best of the human community to the transcendent level of the Body of Christ accomplishing God's purpose and glorifying His Name.

A symphonic orchestra can play great music on its own because of gifted instrumentalists who own the score, but if it is to soar into the realm of the artistic vision, it needs the conductor. Applying this lesson to the potential of the Christ-centered organization, a board of gifted volunteers who are committed to the mission can excel as a working body. However, if the board is to rise to its spiritual potential, it needs a chair who brings the personal experience of Pentecost to the leadership of the board.

Again, as the conductor of an orchestra spends hours of preparation memorizing the score and imagining its artistic fulfillment, the board chair understands the details of the holy text, feels the pulse-beat of the spiritual tone, and brings the impulse of the Holy Spirit to the board meeting. Advance preparation will not only mean personal time in the presence of God seeking the mind of the Holy Spirit, but also sharing time with the chief executive in prayer and reflection over the text and tone of the meeting. Naturally, then, the chair makes devotional time in the board meeting for more than a perfunctory acknowledge of the presence of God. Pentecost is contagious, and the chair is the one who can lead the board into that celebrating community by the infectious influence of personal experience.

Make no mistake—more often than not, the board meetings that I chaired were routine, repetitious, and downright boring. But one meeting will never be forgotten. After working through a contentious issue with wide differences of opinion, we stopped for silence and prayer seeking the mind of Christ. As we lifted our heads, a spirit of unity swept through our ranks, and we were surprised by the speed of action taking us to consensus. Wonder and awe filled the room. Then it happened. Like a standing ovation and shouts of "Bravo" at a concert when the orchestra lifts the audience to a transforming musical experience, our board spontaneously broke out singing the Doxology and rose together in honor of the transcendent presence of the holy God.

Two words describe this moment when transformation gave way to transcendence. One word is *reconciliation*, when all of our differences merge into the mind of Christ and we truly become a community of one accord. The other word is *redemption*, when we realize that the Holy Spirit puts together all of the disparate pieces of the agenda and creates something through us that is very good. It is the moment when the work of the board is recorded as a chapter in redemptive history. It is the moment when the call of the chair is confirmed and the time when the leader of the board stands to join its members singing, "Praise God from whom all blessings flow."

# ENDNOTES

**Chapter 2**

[1] Tyson, John R. *The Way of the Wesleys* (Grand Rapids: Wm. B. Eerdman's Publishing Company, 2014) 119.

**Chapter 3**

[2] McKenna, David L. *Power to Follow, Grace to Lead*. (Waco: Word Books, 1986) 94.

**Chapter 4**

[3] Busby, Dan. *TRUST: The Firm Foundation for Kingdom Fruitfulness*. (Winchester, VA: ECFAPress, 2015) 37.

**Chapter 7**

[4] Carver, John. *Boards that Make a Difference: A New Design for Leaders in Nonprofit and Public Organizations* (San Francisco: Jossey-Bass, 3rd Edition, 2006) 20ff.

[5] Ibid.

[6] Belbin, R. Meredith. *Team Roles at Work* (New York: Taylor and Francis, 2010) 64.

[7] Tozer, A. W. *The Pursuit of God*. (Millenium Publications, 2014), 31.

[8] Egolf, Donald B. *Forming, Storming, Norming, Performing: Successful Communication in Groups and Teams*, 3rd ed. (Bloomington: iUniverse, 2001) 105ff.

## Chapter 8

[9] Fisher, Roger, William Ury. *Getting to Yes: Negotiating Agreement without Giving In* (New York: Penquin Group, 2011) 73.

## Chapter 10

[10] Tolstoy, Leo, *Anna Karenina* (New York: Modern Library Classics, 2000) 1.

[11] Lencioni, Patrick, *The Five Dysfunctions of a Team: A Leadership Fable* (San Francisco: Jossey-Bass, 2002) 188ff.

[12] Tuchman, Barbara W. *The March of Folly: From Troy to Vietnam* (New York: Random House, 2014) 40.

[13] Ibid., 8.

[14] Ibid., 98.

## Chapter 11

[15] Nierenberg, Roger, *Maestro: A Surprising Story About Leading by Listening* (London: Portfolio, 2009).

[16] Ibid., 22.

[17] Ibid., 57.

[18] Ibid., 16ff.

[19] Ibid., 52.

[20] DePree, Max. *Leadership Is an Art* (New York: Dell Publishing, 1989) 11.

[21] Nierenberg, *Maestro*, 30.

[22] Ibid., 86.

[23] Ibid.

[24] Ibid., 35.

[25] Ibid., 82ff.

[26] Ibid., 43ff.

[27] DePree, *Leadership*. Loc.cit.

# ACKNOWLEDGMENTS

No book is written by a single author. The experiences cited and the lessons learned always include coauthors who deserve credit. For this reason, I dedicate this book to the board chairs who were mentors as well as colleagues throughout my career as a chief executive. Hugh White and Glenn White at Spring Arbor College and University, Paul Walls at Seattle Pacific University, and Ira Gallaway and Maxie Dunnam at Asbury Theological Seminary are all remembered as teachers of and learners with me. As a board chair myself, I also acknowledge the chief executives with whom I learned—James Chapman and Gayle Beebe at Spring Arbor University and Ray Bakke and Gwen Dewey at Bakke Graduate University.

I would also like to thank resource leaders in board development who read the manuscript and offered words of wisdom based on their own experience: Gayle Beebe, President of Westmont College; Norman Edwards, Fundraising Consultant and President of BoardWise; David Goodnight, Board Chair of the Free Methodist Foundation; Al Lopus, President of The Best Christian Workplace Institute; and Matthew Whitehead, Board Chair of Seattle Pacific University.

Thanks also to Dan Busby, President of the Evangelical Council for Financial Accountability, who encouraged me to write and agreed to publish the manuscript as a primary resource for his member institutions. His plan to make  complimentary copies available to the board chairs of over 3,000 Christ-centered ministries is an unexpected honor for which I am most grateful.

How can I ever forget the scores of board members, chief executives, administrators, and staff members who added so many dimensions of insight, criticism, and affirmation to my learning? Under no circumstances are they just remembered as "other people." I only wish that I had listened more and talked less. More often than not, their words are wise.

Finally, as always, I acknowledge my wife Jan, who deserves a gold medal for winning the marathon of an author's wife—sitting quietly as I write, waiting for hours until I finish, and encouraging me to keep going when I hit the "writer's wall." Sixty-six years of marriage celebrate her patience and confirm her commitment.


David L. McKenna

# OTHER BOOKS
# BY DAVID L. MCKENNA

*The Jesus Model*

*The Communicator's Commentary: Mark*

*MegaTruth: The Church in the Age of Information*

*Power to Follow, Grace to Lead*

*The Communicator's Commentary: Job*

*The Coming Great Awakening*

*When Our Parents Need Us Most*

*The Communicator's Commentary: Isaiah 1-39*

*The Communicator's Commentary: Isaiah 40-66*

*What a Time to be a Wesleyan: Anticipating the 21st Century*

*How to Read a Christian Book*

*Never Blink in a Hailstorm and Other Lessons of Leadership*

*Becoming Nehemiah*

*A Leader's Legacy: The Gift of Greater Things*

*Stewards of a Sacred Trust: CEO Selection, Transition and Development for Boards of Christ-centered Organizations*

*Christ-centered Leadership: The Incarnational Difference*

*The Succession Principle: How Leaders Make Leaders*

# BOOKS FROM ECFAPress

## Stewards of a Sacred Trust: *CEO Selection, Transition and Development for Boards of Christ-centered Organizations*

by Dr. David McKenna

Transitions are often some of the most important events in our individual lives and the lives of the organizations we serve. When a CEO transition takes place, there is great risk of something going radically wrong. It can affect ministries negatively for years, if not decades.

This thoughtful book is full of wisdom to help ministries steward leadership selection and transition. There are few others who have given such careful thought to these principles and practices.

## The Sower: *Redefining the Ministry of Raising Kingdom Resources*

by Scott Rodin and Gary Hoag

The purpose of this book is to provide momentum to a movement aimed at the heart of every person who is involved in the process of raising money or giving money for the work of God's Kingdom. You may be a full-time development officer, an executive director, a pastor, a president, a board member, a volunteer or a faithful giver. You may have decades of experience in fund development, or this may be the first exposure to this topic. If you care about giving or raising money for God's work, this book is for you.

## The Choice: *The Christ-Centered Pursuit of Kingdom Outcomes*

by Scott Rodin, Gary Hoag, Wesley Willmer

There is the continual push for higher and greater results. When we idolize results that we think please Him, we actually fail to exhibit the obedience He asks of us.

So what should ministry look like? Jesus instructs us to follow Him. This is the Kingdom path.

If this sounds oversimplified, we think we are the ones who have complicated things. Jesus recruited ordinary, mostly uneducated people and gave them basic instructions. He used words like "follow," "trust," and "obey." When we pursue the Kingdom path, then fruitfulness is the by-product. The Kingdom path is the only path that leads to Kingdom outcomes.

## TRUST: *The Firm Foundation for Kingdom Fruitfulness*

by Dan Busby

This book is about trust—the kind of trust with the power of a rolling ocean wave—building a tsunami of goodwill for churches and ministries—and, more importantly, for Christ, our Savior.

If we expect believers to be obedient in their stewardship of their time and talents—including biblical care of the poor and needy, and sharing Jesus Christ with the unreached people groups—it will require a strong demonstration of truth-producing, absolute trust. We need the kind of trust that will catch the attention of the world at large, just as it did in the time of the early church.

To do our part in fulfilling the Great Commission, Trust is the firm foundation for Kingdom fruitfulness.

# GOVERNANCE TOOLBOX
# DIGITAL SERIES

### Just-In-Time Help and Inspiration!

## SHORT VIDEO + 10 MINUTE DISCUSSION = ENGAGEMENT

SERIES No. 1

**RECRUITING BOARD MEMBERS**

SERIES No. 2

**BALANCING BOARD ROLES**

SERIES No. 3

**CONFLICTS OF INTEREST**

SERIES No. 4

**SUCCESSION PLANNING**

**ENGAGE YOUR BOARD AT EVERY MEETING!**
**WATCH FOR NEW SERIES TITLES TO INSPIRE & EQUIP YOUR BOARD**

## HOW TO ACCESS?

**Each Toolbox includes:**
1 online video,
**Board Member Read-and-Engage Viewing Guide** *(pdf download)* **and**
**Facilitator Guide** *(pdf download)*

## ORDER RESOURCES FROM: ECFA.ORG/TOOLBOX

## VIEW • INSPIRE • ENGAGE!

## The Guide to Charitable Giving
## for Churches and Ministries

*A practical resource on how to handle gifts with integrity*

by Dan Busby, Michael Martin, John Van Drunen

*The Guide to Charitable Giving for Churches and Ministries* will be your one-stop resource covering the legal, tax, accounting, and integrity issues related to charitable giving.

In this easy-to-understand guide, you will learn about issues such as ministry communications and gift acknowledgments, giver-restricted gifts, and contributions to support missionaries.

# RECOMMENDED BOOKS

Zondervan
## Church and Nonprofit
*Tax & Financial Guide*

Zondervan
## Minister's
*Tax & Financial Guide*

**Dan Busby**
**Michael Martin**
**John Van Drunen**

Ministers and churches can use these award-winning tax guides from Zondervan to comply with federal tax laws. These guides go beyond other tax guides because they provide:

- ☑ complete tax and financial guides for ministers, churches, and nonprofit organizations

- ☑ recent and last-minute changes in this year's tax laws

- ☑ easy-to-follow explanations (in plain English)

- ☑ help in taking advantage of favorable tax laws

- ☑ sound advice for future planning

- ☑ money-saving tax strategies (now and for the future)

- ☑ sample forms and worksheets